Author's Preface

The title of this book is a question; and that question, as far as the Western world is concerned, has been given some dubious and suspect answers in recent years. Moreover the rapidly expanding interest in Sufism increases still further the need for a reliable introductory book—introductory in the sense that it requires no special knowledge, and reliable in that it is not written any more simply than truth will allow.

But though such a book may presuppose no special knowledge, it necessarily presupposes a deep and searching interest in spiritual things. More particularly, it presupposes at least an inkling of the possibility of direct inward perception—an inkling that may become a seed of aspiration. Or at the very least, it presupposes that the soul shall not be closed to this possibility. Nearly 1000 years ago a great Sufi defined Sufism as 'taste', because its aim and its end could be summed up as direct knowledge of transcendent truths, such knowledge being, insofar as its directness is concerned, more comparable to the experiences of the senses than to mental knowledge.

Most Western readers of this book will have heard quite early in life that 'the Kingdom of Heaven is within you'. They will also have heard the words: 'Seek and ye shall find; knock and it shall be opened unto you'. But how many of them have ever received any instruction in the way of seeking or the art of knocking? And even as these last four words were being written down, it came to mind that they are, in this given context, an answer to the very question put by our title.

Enough has now been said to make it clear that although our subject may be treated summarily—a book of this size, for so vast a theme, is bound to be summary—it cannot be treated superficially, for that would amount to a contradiction in terms. Sufism is a touchstone, an implacable criterion which reduces everything else, except its own equivalents, to a flat surface of two dimensions only, being itself the real dimension of height and of depth.

MARTIN LINGS
London 1973

What is Sufism?

Also by Martin Lings

Ancient Beliefs and Modern Superstitions

Shakespeare in the Light of Sacred Art

The Elements and other Poems

The Book of Certainty
(The Sufi Doctrine of Faith, Vision and Gnosis)

A Sufi Saint of the Twentieth Century: Shaikh Aḥmad Al-ʻAlawī
(second edition, revised and enlarged, of *A Moslem Saint*)

The Heralds and other Poems

The Quranic Art of Calligraphy and Illumination

What is Sufism?

MARTIN LINGS

UNIVERSITY OF CALIFORNIA PRESS
Berkeley and Los Angeles

UNIVERSITY OF CALIFORNIA PRESS
Berkeley and Los Angeles, California

First California Paperback Edition, 1977

ISBN 0-520-03171-7

Printed in the United States of America 1 2 3 4 5 6 7 8 9 0

Contents

Chapter 1

The Originality of Sufism

The great Andalusian Sufi, Muhyi 'd-Dīn Ibn 'Arabī, used to pray a prayer which begins: 'Enter me, O Lord, into the deep of the Ocean of Thine Infinite Oneness',[1] and in the treatises of the Sufis this 'Ocean' is mentioned again and again, likewise by way of symbolic reference to the End towards which their path is directed. Let us therefore begin by saying, on the basis of this symbol, in answer to the question 'What is Sufism?': From time to time a Revelation 'flows' like a great tidal wave from the Ocean of Infinitude to the shores of our finite world; and Sufism is the vocation and the discipline and the science of plunging into the ebb of one of these waves and being drawn back with it to its Eternal and Infinite Source.

'From time to time': this is a simplification which calls for a commentary; for since there is no common measure between the origin of such a wave and its destination, its temporality is bound to partake, mysteriously, of the Eternal, just as its finiteness is bound to partake of the Infinite. Being temporal, it must first reach this world at a certain moment in history; but that moment will in a sense escape from time. *Better than a thousand months*[2] is how the Islamic Revelation describes the night of its own advent. There must also be an end which

[1] British Museum Ms. Or. 13453 (3).

[2] *Qur'ān* XCVII: 3.

corresponds to the beginning; but that end will be too remote to be humanly foreseeable. Divine institutions are made *for ever*.[3] Another imprint of the Eternal Present upon it will be that it is always flowing and always ebbing in the sense that it has, virtually, both a flow and an ebb for every individual that comes within its scope.

There is only one water, but no two Revelations are outwardly the same. Each wave has its own characteristics according to its destination, that is, the particular needs of time and place towards which and in response to which it has providentially been made to flow. These needs, which include all kinds of ethnic receptivities and aptitudes such as vary from people to people, may be likened to the cavities and hollows which lie in the path of the wave. The vast majority of believers are exclusively concerned with the water which the wave deposits in these receptacles and which constitutes the formal aspect of the religion.

Mystics on the other hand—and Sufism is a kind of mysticism—are by definition concerned above all with 'the mysteries of the Kingdom of Heaven'; and it would therefore be true to say, in pursuance of our image, that the mystic is one who is consequently more preoccupied by the ebbing wave than by the water which it has left behind. He has none the less need of this residue like the rest of his community—need, that is, of the outward forms of his religion which concern the human individual as such. For if it be asked what is it in the mystic that can ebb with the ebbing wave, part of the answer will be: not his body and not his soul. The body cannot ebb until the Resurrection, which is the first stage of the reabsorption of the body—and with it the whole material state—into the higher states of being. As to the soul, it has to wait until the death of the body. Until then, though immortal, it is imprisoned in the world of mortality. At the death of Ghazālī, the great eleventh-century Sufi, a poem which he had written

[3] *Exodus* XII: 14.

in his last illness was found beneath his head. In it are the lines:

> A bird I am: this body was my cage
> But I have flown leaving it as a token.[4]

Other great Sufis also have said what amounts to the same: but they have also made it clear in their writing or speaking or living—and this is, for us, the measure of their greatness—that something in them had already ebbed before death despite the 'cage', something incomparably more important than anything that has to wait for death to set it free.

What is drawn back by spiritual realisation towards the Source might be called the centre of consciousness. The Ocean is within as well as without; and the path of the mystics is a gradual awakening as it were 'backwards' in the direction of the root of one's being, a remembrance of the Supreme Self which infinitely transcends the human ego and which is none other than the Deep towards which the wave ebbs.

To use a very different image which will help to complete the first, let us liken this world to a garden—or more precisely, to a nursery garden, for there is nothing in it that has not been planted there with a view to its being eventually transplanted elsewhere. The central part of the garden is allotted to trees of a particularly noble kind, though relatively small and growing in earthenware pots; but as we look at them, all our attention is caught by one that is arrestingly finer than any of the others, which it far excels in luxuriance and vigour of growth. The cause is not naked to the eye, but we know at once what has happened, without the need for any investigation: the tree has somehow been able to strike root deep into the earth through the base of its receptacle.

The trees are souls, and that tree of trees is one who, as the Hindus say, has been 'liberated in life', one who has

[4] British Museum Ms. Or. 7561, f. 86. The whole poem is translated in Margaret Smith's *Al-Ghazālī the Mystic* (Luzac, 1944), pp. 36–7.

realised what the Sufis term 'the Supreme Station;' and Sufism is a way and a means of striking a root through the 'narrow gate' in the depth of the soul out into the domain of the pure and unimprisonable Spirit which itself opens out on to the Divinity. The full-grown Sufi is thus conscious of being, like other men, a prisoner in the world of forms, but unlike them he is also conscious of being free, with a freedom which immeasurably outweighs his imprisonment. He may therefore be said to have two centres of consciousness, one human and one Divine, and he may speak now from one and now from the other, which accounts for certain apparent contradictions.

To follow the path of the mystics is to acquire as it were an extra dimension, for this path is nothing other than the dimension of depth.[5] Consequently, as will be seen in more detail later, even those rites which the mystic shares with the rest of his community, and which he too needs for the balance of his soul, are not performed by him exoterically as others perform them, but from the same profound esoteric point of view which characterises all his rites and which he is methodically forbidden to forsake. In other words he must not lose sight of the truth that the water which is left behind by the wave is the same water as that which ebbs. Analogously, he must not forget that his soul, like the water that is 'imprisoned' in forms, is not essentially different from the transcendent Spirit, of which it is a prolongation, like a hand that is held out and inserted into a receptacle and then, eventually, withdrawn.

If the reason for the title of this chapter is not yet apparent, this is partly because the word 'original' has become encrusted

[5] Or of height, which is the complementary aspect of the same dimension. The Tree of Life, of which the Saint is a personification, is sometimes depicted as having its roots in Heaven, lest it should be forgotten that depth and height are spiritually identical.

with meanings which do not touch the essence of originality but which are limited to one of its consequences, namely difference, the quality of being unusual or extraordinary. 'Original' is even used as a synonym of 'abnormal' which is a monstrous perversion, since true originality is always a norm. Nor can it be achieved by the will of man, whereas the grotesque is doubly easy to achieve, precisely because it is no more than a chaos of borrowings.

The original is that which springs directly from the origin or source, like pure uncontaminated water which has not undergone any 'side' influences. Originality is thus related to inspiration, and above all to revelation, for the origins are transcendent, being beyond this world, in the domain of the Spirit. Ultimately the origin is no less than the Absolute, the Infinite and the Eternal—whence the Divine Name 'The Originator', in Arabic *al-Badī'*, which can also be translated 'the Marvellous'. It is from this Ocean of Infinite Possibility that the great tidal waves of Revelation flow, each 'marvellously' different from the others because each bears the imprint of the One-and-Only from which it springs, this imprint being the quality of uniqueness, and each profoundly the same because the essential content of its message is the One-and-Only Truth.

In the light of the image of the wave we see that originality is a guarantee of both authenticity and effectuality. Authenticity, of which orthodoxy is as it were the earthly face, is constituted by the flow of the wave, that is, the direct provenance of the Revelation from its Divine Origin; and in every flow there is the promise of an ebb, wherein lies effectuality, the Grace of the Truth's irresistible power of attraction.

Sufism is nothing other than Islamic mysticism, which means that it is the central and most powerful current of that tidal wave which constitutes the Revelation of Islam; and it will be clear from what has just been said that to affirm this is in no sense a depreciation, as some appear to think. It is on the contrary an affirmation that Sufism is both authentic and effectual.

As to the thousands of men and women in the modern Western world who, while claiming to be 'Sufis', maintain that Sufism is independent of any particular religion and that it has always existed, they unwittingly reduce it—if we may use the same elemental image—to a network of artificial inland waterways. They fail to notice that by robbing it of its particularity and therefore of its originality, they also deprive it of all impetus. Needless to say, the waterways exist. For example, ever since Islam established itself in the subcontinent of India, there have been intellectual exchanges between Sufis and Brahmins; and Sufism eventually came to adopt certain terms and notions from Neoplatonism. But the foundations of Sufism were laid and its subsequent course irrevocably fixed long before it would have been possible for extraneous and parallel mystical influences to have introduced non-Islamic elements, and when such influences were finally felt, they touched only the surface.

In other words, by being totally dependent upon one particular Revelation, Sufism is totally independent of everything else. But while being self-sufficient it can, if time and place concur, pluck flowers from gardens other than its own. The Prophet of Islam said: 'Seek knowledge even if it be in China'.

Chapter 2

The Universality of Sufism

Those who insist that Sufism is 'free from the shackles of religion'[1] do so partly because they imagine that its universality is at stake. But however sympathetic we may feel towards their preoccupation with this undoubted aspect of Sufism, it must not be forgotten that particularity is perfectly compatible with universality, and in order to perceive this truth in an instant we have only to consider sacred art, which is both unsurpassably particular and unsurpassably universal.[2] To take the example nearest our theme, Islamic art is immediately recognizable as such in virtue of its distinctness from any other sacred art: 'Nobody will deny the unity of Islamic art, either in time or in space; it is far too evident: whether one contemplates the mosque of Cordova or the great madrasah of Samarkand, whether it be the tomb of a saint in the Maghreb or one in Chinese Turkestan, it is as if one and the same light shone forth from all these works of art.'[3] At the same time, such is

[1] So it is in a way, but not in the way that they have in mind.

[2] This emerges with clarity from Titus Burckhardt's *Sacred Art in East and West: its Principles and Methods* (Perennial Books, London, 1967), as does also the close relationship between sacred art and mysticism.

[3] Titus Burckhardt, 'Perennial Values in Islamic Art' in *Studies in Comparative Religion* (Summer, 1967).

the universality of the great monuments of Islam that in the presence of any one of them we have the impression of being at the centre of the world.[4]

Far from being a digression, the question of sacred art brings us back to our central theme, for in response to the question 'What is Sufism?', a possible answer—on condition that other answers were also forthcoming—would be simply to point to the Taj Mahal or to some other masterpiece of Islamic architecture. Nor would a potential Sufi fail to understand this answer, for the aim and end of Sufism is sainthood, and all sacred art in the true and full sense of the term is as a crystallisation of sanctity, just as a Saint is as an incarnation of some holy monument, both being manifestations of the Divine Perfection.

According to Islamic doctrine, Perfection is a synthesis of the Qualities of Majesty and Beauty; and Sufism, as many Sufis have expressed it, is a putting on of these Divine Qualities, which means divesting the soul of the limitations of fallen man, the habits and prejudices which have become 'second nature', and investing it with the characteristics of man's primordial nature, made in the image of God. Thus it is that the rite of initiation into some Sufi orders actually takes the form of an investiture: a mantle (*khirqah*) is placed by the Shaykh over the shoulders of the initiate.

The novice takes on the way of life of the adept, for part of the method of all mysticisms—and of none more than Islamic mysticism—is to anticipate the end; the adept continues the way of life he took on as novice. The difference

[4] This idea has been borrowed from Frithjof Schuon's masterly demonstration of the difference between sacred art and art which is religious without being sacred. I have also taken the liberty of transposing it from its Christian setting. The original is as follows: 'When standing in front of a Romanesque or Gothic cathedral, we feel that we are at the centre of the world; when standing in front of a Renaissance, Baroque or Rococo church we are merely conscious of being in Europe.' (*The Transcendent Unity of Religions*, p. 84).

between the two is that in the case of the adept the way, that is, Sufism, has become altogether spontaneous, for sainthood has triumphed over 'second nature'. In the case of the novice the way is, to begin with, mainly a discipline. But sacred art is as a Divine Grace which can make easy what is difficult. Its function—and this is the supreme function of art—is to precipitate in the soul a victory for sainthood, of which the masterpiece in question is an image. As a complement to discipline—we might even say as a respite—it presents the path as one's natural vocation in the literal sense, summoning together all the souls' elements for an act of unanimous assent to the Perfection which it manifests.

If it be asked: Could we not equally well point to the Temple of Hampi or to the Cathedral of Chartres as to the Taj Mahal as a crystallisation of Sufism? the answer will be a 'yes' outweighed by a 'no'. Both the Hindu temple and the Christian cathedral are supreme manifestations of Majesty and Beauty, and a would-be Sufi who failed to recognise them and rejoice in them as such would be falling short of his qualification inasmuch as he would be failing to give the signs of God their due. But it must be remembered that sacred art is for every member of the community in which it flowers, and that it represents not only the end but also the means and the perspective or, in other words, the way opening onto the end; and neither the temple nor the cathedral was destined to display the ideals of Islam and to reveal it as a means to the end as were the great mosques and, on another plane, the great Sufis. It would certainly not be impossible to point out the affinity between the particular modes of Majesty and Beauty which are manifested in both these Islamic exemplars, that is, in the static stone perfections and in their dynamic living counterparts. But such an analysis of what might be called the perfume of Islamic spirituality would be beyond the scope of a book of this nature. Suffice it to say that the Oneness of the Truth is reflected in all its

Revelations not only by the quality of uniqueness but also by that of homogeneity. Thus each of the great theocratic civilisations is a unique and homogeneous whole, differing from all the others as one fruit differs from another and 'tasting' the same all through, in all its different aspects. The Muslim mystic can thus give himself totally, without any reserve,[5] to a great work of Islamic art; and if it be a shrine he can, by entering it, put it on as the raiment of sanctity and wear it as an almost organic prolongation of the Sufism which it has helped to triumph in his soul. The same triumph could be furthered by the temple or the cathedral; but he could not 'wear' either of these—at least, not until he had actually transcended all forms by spiritual realisation which is very different from a merely theoretic understanding.

Sacred art was mentioned in that it provides an immediately obvious example of the compatibility between the universal and the particular. The same compatibility is shown by the symbolism of the circle with its centre, its radii, and its circumference. The word 'symbolism' is used here to show that the circle is being considered not as an arbitrary image but as a form which is rooted in the reality it illustrates, in the sense that it owes its existence to that reality, of which it is in fact an existential prolongation. If the Truth were not Radiant there could be no such thing as a radius, not even a geometric one, let alone a spiritual path which is the highest example. All radii would vanish from existence; and with this vanishing the universe itself would vanish, for the radius is

[5] That is, without fear of receiving any alien vibration, for two spiritual perspectives can be, for doctrinal or methodic reasons, mutually exclusive in some of their aspects while converging on the same end. But sacred art is an auxiliary and does not normally constitute a central means of spiritual realisation. Any danger that might come from the sacred art of a traditional line other than one's own is thus incomparably less than the dangers inherent in practising the rites of another religion. Such a violation of spiritual homogeneity could cause a shock powerful enough to unbalance the soul.

one of the greatest of all symbols inasmuch as it symbolises that on which everything depends, namely the connection between the Divine Principle and its manifestations or creations.

Everyone is conscious of 'being at a point' or of 'having reached a point', even if this be no more than consciousness of having reached a certain age. Mysticism begins with the consciousness that this point is on a radius. It then proceeds by what might be described as an exploitation of this fact, the radius being a Ray of Divine Mercy which emanates from the Supreme Centre and leads back to it. The point must now become a point of Mercy. In other words, there must be a deliberate realisation or actualisation of the Mercy inherent in the point which is the only part of the radius which one can as yet command. This means taking advantage of those possibilities of Mercy which are immediately available, namely the outer formal aspects of religion which, though always within reach, may have been lying entirely neglected or else only made use of exoterically, that is, considering the point in isolation without reference to the radius as a whole.

The radius itself is the religion's dimension of mysticism; thus, in the case of Islam, it is Sufism, which is seen in the light of this symbol to be both particular and universal—particular in that it is distinct from each of the other radii which represent other mysticisms and universal because, like them, it leads to the One Centre. Our image as a whole reveals clearly the truth that as each mystical path approaches its End it is nearer to the other mysticisms than it was at the beginning.[6] But there is a complementary and almost paradoxical

[6] It reveals also, incidentally, the ineffectuality of dilettantism, which corresponds to a meandering line that sometimes moves towards the centre and sometimes away from it, crossing and recrossing various radii but following none with any constancy while claiming to follow a synthesis of all. The self-deceivers in question are, to quote a Sufi of the last century (the Shaykh ad-Darqāwī) 'like a man who tries to find water

truth which it cannot reveal,[7] but which it implies by the idea of concentration which it evokes: increase of nearness does not mean decrease of distinctness, for the nearer the centre, the greater the concentration, and the greater the concentration, the stronger the 'dose'. The concentrated essence of Islam is only to be found in the Sufi Saint who, by reaching the End of the Path, has carried the particular ideals of his religion to their highest and fullest development, just as the concentrated essence of Christianity is only to be found in a St Francis or a St Bernard or a St Dominic. In other words, not only the universality but also the originality of each particular mysticism increases in intensity as the End is approached. Nor could it be otherwise inasmuch as originality is inseparable from uniqueness, and this, as well as universality, is necessarily increased by nearness to the Oneness which confers it.

While we are on this theme, it should be mentioned that there is a lesser universality as well as the greater one which we have been considering. All mysticisms are equally universal in the greater sense in that they all lead to the One Truth. But one feature of the originality of Islam, and therefore of Sufism, is what might be called a secondary universality, which is to be explained above all by the fact that as the last Revelation of this cycle of time it is necessarily something of a summing up. The Islamic *credo* is expressed by the Qur'ān as belief *in God and His Angels and His Books and His Messengers.*[8] The following passage is also significant in this context.

by digging a little here and a little there and who will die of thirst; whereas a man who digs deep in one spot, trusting in the Lord and relying on Him, will find water; he will drink and give others to drink' (*Letters of a Sufi Master* (Perennial Books, London, 1969) p. 29).

[7] A symbol is by definition fragmentary in that it can never capture all the aspects of its archetype. What escapes it in this instance is the truth that the Centre is infinitely greater than the circumference. It therefore needs to be complemented at the back of our minds by another circle whose centre stands for this world and whose circumference symbolises the All-Surrounding Infinite.

[8] II: 285.

Nothing comparable to it could be found in either Judaism or Christianity, for example: *For each We have appointed a law and a path; and if God*[9] *had wished He would have made you one people. But He hath made you as ye are that He may put you to the test in what He hath given you. So vie with one another in good works. Unto God ye will all be brought back and He will then tell you about those things wherein ye differed.*[10] Moreover—and this is why one speaks of a 'cycle' of time—there is a certain coincidence between the last and the first. With Islam 'the wheel has come full circle', or almost; and that is why it claims to be a return to the primordial religion, which gives it yet another aspect of universality. One of the characteristics of the Qur'ān as the last Revelation is that at times it becomes as it were transparent in order that the first Revelation may shine through its verses; and this first Revelation, namely the Book of Nature, belongs to everyone. Out of deference to this Book the miracles of Muhammad, unlike those of Moses and Jesus, are never allowed to hold the centre of the stage. That, in the Islamic perspective, must be reserved for the great miracle of creation which, with the passage of time, is taken more and more for granted and which needs to be restored to its original status. In this connection it is not irrelevant to mention that one of the sayings of the Prophet that is most often quoted by the Sufis is the following 'Holy Tradition', (*ḥadīth qudusī*),[11] so called because in it God speaks directly: 'I was a Hidden Treasure and I wished to be known, and so I created the world.'

[9] The Qur'ān speaks with the voice of the Divinity not only in the first person (both singular and plural) but also in the third person, sometimes changing from one to the other in two consecutive sentences as here.

[10] V: 48.

[11] The word 'Tradition' will be used throughout with a capital letter when it translates *ḥadīth*, literally 'a handed-down saying' (by the Prophet himself or by one of his Companions, with reference to him).

It is no doubt in virtue of these and other aspects of universality that the Qur'ān says, addressing the whole community of Muslims: *We have made you a middle people*;[12] and it will perhaps be seen from the following chapters, though without there being any aim to demonstrate this, that Sufism is in fact something of a bridge between East and West.

[12] II: 143.

Chapter 3

The Book

If it be asked, with reference to our basic symbolism, what form does the tidal wave take, the answer is that it takes above all the form of a book, namely the Qur'ān. The Sufis speak of 'seeking to be drowned' (*istighrāq*) in the verses of the Qur'ān which are, according to one of the most fundamental doctrines of Islam, the Uncreated Word of God.[1] What they are seeking is, to use another Sufi term, extinction (*fanā'*) of the created in the Uncreated, of the temporal in the Eternal, of the finite in the Infinite; and for some Sufis the recitation of the Qur'ān has been, throughout life, their chief means of concentration upon God which is itself the essence of every spiritual path. It is even read continuously by some Sufis—in India and West Africa, for example—who know very little Arabic; and if it be objected that such a reading can have only a fragmentary effect upon the soul inasmuch as the minds of the readers will be excluded from participation, the answer is that their minds are penetrated by the consciousness that they are partaking of the Divine Word. Their reading thus becomes the equivalent of a long drawn-out invocation of the Name

[1] Like Hinduism and Judaism, Islam makes a clear distinction between Revelation and inspiration. A Revelation is consubstantial with the Divinity of which it is as a projection or prolongation, whereas an inspired text is composed by man under the influence of the Divine Spirit. In Christianity the Revelation is Jesus himself, the Gospels being at the degree of inspiration.

Allāh. Moreover they are conscious that the Qur'ān is a flow and an ebb—that it flows to them from God and that its verses are miraculous signs (*āyāt*) which will take them back to God, and that is precisely why they read it.

The text itself confirms this attitude, for if the theme of the Qur'ān is above all Allāh Himself, its secondary theme is that it comes directly from Him by way of Revelation and that it leads back to Him through guidance along *the straight path.* Immediately after the seven opening verses the main body of the Quranic text begins with an affirmation of this authenticity and effectuality: *Alif-Lām-Mīm—that, beyond doubt, is the book—a guidance for the pious.* The first of the initial letters stands for *Allāh*, the second for *Rasūl*,[2] Messenger, that is, the heavenly nature of the Prophet, and the third for *Muḥammad* which is the name of his earthly nature. In virtue of the continuity they represent, these letters trace out the flow of the wave, *guidance* being its ebb. The same authenticity and effectuality are affirmed by the two names of Mercy, *ar-Raḥmān* and *ar-Raḥīm*, with which the chapters of the Qur'ān begin. The first of the two signifies above all the Ocean Itself in its aspect of Infinite Goodness and Beauty, which by its nature is overflowing; *ar-Raḥmān* may therefore, by extension, be taken to signify also the flow of the wave, the Mercy which creates and reveals and sends forth angelic and human Messengers. Such words as *We have revealed it* or *We have sent thee (Muhammad) as Messenger* are a constant refrain throughout the Quranic text. No less recurrent are those verses which affirm the attraction of the Infinite, the Mercy of *ar-Raḥīm* which draws man back to his Origin, enabling him to transcend his human and terrestrial limitations, verses such as *Verily God is the*

[2] In Arabic the final as well as the initial radical letter can stand for the whole word. Sometimes the letter *Lām* is interpreted in this context as signifying *Jibrīl*, the Archangel Gabriel, who brought the Revelation to Muhammad.

All-Forgiving, the All-Merciful[3] or *God summoneth whom He will unto the Abode of Peace* or *Unto Him is the ultimate becoming* or the injunction *Respond unto the call of God* or the question *Do not all things return to God?* The Qur'ān is penetrated by finality; and in particular, as the last scripture of the cycle, it is haunted by *the Hour*, the sudden end which *weighs heavily in the womb of the heavens and the earth*,[4] and the mention of which is a refrain which complements that of creation and revelation.

The Islamic Revelation embraces every aspect of human life, leaving absolutely nothing to 'Caesar'; and by the law of concordant actions and reactions the fullness of its flow into this world finds its reactions in the far-reachingness of its ebb, the depth to which it returns in the domain of metaphysical truth. In certain passages it reaches a level which infinitely transcends the duality of Creator and created, Lord and slave, and which is no less than the degree of the Divine Essence Itself.[5]

The Qur'ān is the book of the whole community, yet at the same time, and above all, it is the book of a minority, the book of a spiritual elect. It achieves this double aspect in different ways. Firstly, it is full of 'open' verses which every believer can and indeed must apply to himself or herself but which may none the less be said to apply pre-eminently to the Sufis. For example, the supplication contained in the *Fātiḥah*, the opening chapter, is: *Guide us along the straight path.* This occurs several times in the ritual prayer and is consequently the most often repeated supplication in Islam. Yet it 'belongs' especially to the Sufis because, being by far the most 'path-

[3] The Name *ar-Raḥīm* is most often preceded in the Qur'ān by *al-Ghafūr*, the All-Forgiving.

[4] VII: 187.

[5] Not that any Revelation can fall short of this level. Christianity for example reaches it implicitly, just as it implicitly embraces the whole of life. But the Qur'ān does both explicitly.

minded' members of the community, they can give themselves to this verse as no others can, entering into it as into their own element. Moreover, they alone do justice to the superlative implicit in the definite article. In general, the mystic could be defined as one who has asked himself the question: 'What is the straightest path?' It is as an answer to this question that Sufism exists, and for no other reason, for it is by definition the way of most direct approach to God, so much so that the word *ṭarīqah*[6] (way) has by extension the meaning of Sufi order or brotherhood.

Another comparable verse, greatly beloved for its outstanding beauty as well as for its meaning, and recited by all, especially in times of stress, is the verse of 'seeking to return' (*istirjā'*): *Verily we are for God and verily unto Him we are returning.*[7] The Sufis claim that the whole of Sufism is summed up in this verse, and it is often chanted at their gatherings and sometimes repeated a certain number of times on a rosary; and in fact, although every believer is necessarily 'for God' in some degree or other, the mystic may be said to be 'for God' in a way which the rest of the community is not, for mysticism implies total dedication. Moreover, as regards both these verses, it must be remembered that Sufism is nothing if not a movement of return, an ebb, and that by the standards of Sufism the rest of the community, although facing in the right direction, is stationary. Even among themselves the Sufis make a distinction between those more central members of an order who are what they call 'travellers' (*sālikūn*) and those more peripheric members who are relatively at a standstill.

Such verses as these can be called 'open' because they may be said to apply to the whole hierarchy of spiritual aspiration in all its different degrees. Nonetheless, the difference between the lowest and the highest degree is enough to constitute a

[6] It is partly synonymous with *ṣirāṭ* (path) but has a wider meaning and could be translated 'way and means'.

[7] *Innā li 'Llāhi wa-innā ilayhi rāji 'ūn*, II: 156.

difference of meaning; and in fact the Prophet said that every verse of the Qur'ān has 'an outside and an inside'. We have just seen two examples of inner meanings. As to the 'outside' of the verses in question, the exoteric 'straight path' is the path of not deviating from the law of Islam, whereas the movement of return in its outermost sense is the passage through a pious life towards death. Both meanings, the outer and the inner, concern the Sufis; but as to the majority, apart from the fact that they are not in general mentally disposed to take in more than one meaning for one set of words, they would have difficulty in understanding what the Sufis mean by 'travel' (*sulūk*), that is, the inward deepening or ebbing of the finite self in the direction of its Divine Principle.

In many verses the outer and inner meanings apply to quite different domains. On one occasion, when returning from a battle against the infidels, the Prophet said: 'We have come back from the lesser Holy War to the Greater Holy War'. His Companions asked: 'What is the Greater Holy War?' and he answered: 'The war against the soul'. Here lies the key to the inner meaning of all those verses in the Qur'ān which refer to Holy War and to the infidels. Admittedly this saying of the Prophet has something for everybody, and most Muslims would claim to have had experience of fighting against the inward infidels, that is, the rebellious non-muslim elements of the soul. But to resist temptation from time to time is one thing and to wage war is another. The Greater Holy War in its full sense is Sufism or, more precisely, it is an aspect of Sufism, and it concerns none but the Sufis. The Qur'ān says: *Wage war on the idolaters totally*[8] and elsewhere *Fight them until there is no longer any sedition, and religion is all for God.*[9] Only the mystic is capable of realising this inwardly, and only he knows what it is to keep up a methodic opposition to his own lower possibilities and to carry the war into the

[8] IX: 36. [9] VIII: 39.

enemy's territory so that the whole soul may be 'for God'. It is on account of the extreme dangers of this war that no true esoterism is easy of access. Exoterism, not deliberately but in fact, is a state of truce with occasional desultory skirmishes; and it is far better to remain an exoterist than to rouse the full fury of the enemy and then to give up the fight, allowing the lower possibilities to overrun the soul.

It would be possible to give a multitude of other examples of inner meanings which concern only the Sufis. But since several of these will come to light in later chapters, it will be enough for the moment to dwell on the general affinity which the Sufis have with the Qur'ān in virtue of what especially distinguishes them from other Muslims, namely that the choice they have deliberately and irrevocably made of the Eternal in preference to the ephemeral is not merely theoretic or mental but so totally sincere that it has shaken them to the depth of their being and set them in motion upon the path. The Qur'ān itself is as a crystallisation of this choice, for it insists without respite on the immense disparity between this lower world and the transcendent world of the Spirit, while on the other hand it continually inveighs against the folly of those who choose the lower in place of the higher, the worse in place of the better. As the opposite of this folly, Sufism could be defined as a sense of values or a sense of proportion. Nor would this be inadequate as a definition, for who in the world, except their counterparts in other religions, can possibly compare with the Sufis for putting first things first and second things second? Analogously, the Qur'ān defines itself as *al-Furqān* which could be translated 'the Criterion of Values' or 'the Instrument of Discrimination' or simply 'Discernment'.

An essential feature of the Quranic message is the establishment of a hierarchy of values which can serve as a criterion for putting everything in its proper place and as a general basis for drawing conclusions. It does not only distinguish between right and wrong, orthodoxy and error, truth and falsehood, religion and paganism. It also makes a distinction, within the domain of orthodoxy, between those who press eagerly forward, *the foremost*, and those who observe a certain moderation in their worship and, parallel to this, if the war in question be interpreted as the Greater Holy War, between those who go out to fight and those who stay behind. Both will receive their reward. *Unto both God hath promised good. But he hath favoured those who fight with an immense reward above those who stay behind.*[10] Another parallel distinction, not necessarily identical, is between *the foremost* who are said to be *near to God* (literally 'brought near', *muqarrabūn*, a word used to distinguish the Archangels from the Angels) and *those on the right*[11] (the infidels being *those on the left*). Elsewhere, on two occasions, the highest category, who are also named the *slaves of God* to denote their extinction in Him, are contrasted with *the righteous*.[12] These last would seem to hold an intermediary rank between *the foremost* and those *on the right*. At any rate, it is significant that *the foremost* are represented as drinking in Paradise directly from its two supreme Fountains, whereas *the righteous* drink from them indirectly, that is they drink a draught which has been flavoured at one or other of these fountains, while *those on the right* drink water. This symbolism, so rich in implications, needs no commentary in the sense that to understand it we have only to look at the Islamic community as it always has been and as it still is today. Whatever subdivisions there may be, the three main divisions of the spiritual hierarchy are, firstly, those Sufis who are 'travellers', secondly, those who are relatively 'stationary' but whose faith and practice are none the less perfumed with Sufism, and thirdly the 'exoteric' majority.

It is true that the 'furqanic' distinctions are for the information of everyone. But no hierarchy can be fully grasped except by those at its top. The Qur'ān establishes this hierarchy

[10] IV: 95. [11] LVI: 8–40.
[12] LXXVI: 5–6; LXXXIII: 18–28.

from above; and the Sufi, in virtue of 'pressing forward' to the summit of the hierarchy is the one who comes nearest to the Quranic standpoint—the nearest to personifying the Furqān.

The theme of this chapter will necessarily overflow into other chapters inasmuch as both the doctrine and the methods of Sufism have their roots in the Qur'ān. But the present context calls for at least a mention of the fact that certain formulations of the Qur'ān would seem to be, even as regards their literal message, for the Sufis and for no one else. We will take here just one example, leaving others to emerge later:

We (God) are nearer to him (man) than his jugular vein.[13] This cannot be called an 'open' verse such as *Guide us along the straight path* which everyone is free to interpret according to his conception of the path and of straightness. Nor is it comparable to those verses whose literal meaning is a veil over a truth that is not for everyone. The 'inside' is here, exceptionally, the literal meaning. The protective 'outside' is simply the dazzlement caused by the sudden unveiling of what is, for man, the truth of truths. The dazzled majority turn their attention to other verses; but for at least some of those who take it literally, this verse leaves no alternative but to go in search of a Sufi Shaykh—a spiritual Master who can unfold the way of living up to such Nearness.

[13] L: 16.

Chapter 4

The Messenger

On one occasion after the death of Muhammad when his favourite wife 'Ā'ishah was asked what he was like, she replied: 'His nature was as the Qur'ān'. This must be taken to mean that from her intense and intimate experience of the Prophet she formed the impression that he was as an incarnation of the revealed Book. Nor is her answer surprising in view of the analogy between the Message and the Messenger, for the Messenger (*rasūl*) is not only the recipient of the Revealed Message but he also, like the Revelation, is 'sent'—that is what *rasūl* means—into this world from the Beyond. The Islamic doctrine of the *Rasūl* is ultimately the same as the Hindu doctrine of the *Avatāra*, the immediate difference being that the term *Avatāra* means 'descent', that is, of the Divinity, whereas the *Rasūl* is defined either as an Archangel or else as a human incarnation of the Spirit. But this difference is one of perspective rather than fact, for the Spirit has an uncreated aspect opening onto the Divinity as well as a created one. The Divinity of the *Rasūl* is veiled by the hierarchy of the spiritual degrees which mark the line of his descent, and the purpose of this veiling is to safeguard the doctrine of the Divine Oneness, whereas in the case of the *Avatāra* the same hierarchy is as it were 'folded up' lest it should blur the identity of self with Self which constitutes the essence of the Hindu doctrine of *Advaita* (Non-duality). This identity is also the essence of

Sufism, but the Sufis tend to express it elliptically except, as we shall see, in their 'inspired ejaculations'.

The most striking aspect of the parallelism between the Qur'ān and Muhammad is no doubt to be seen in their far-reaching penetration, each being suggestive of a wave of great impetus which flows exceptionally far inland. Just as the Qur'ān embraces every aspect of human life, so it was the destiny of Muhammad to penetrate with exceptional versatility into the domain of human experience, both public and private.[1] The ebb corresponds to the flow: the earthly plenitude of the Prophet is combined with an extreme sensitivity to the magnetism of the Hereafter; and this combination has left an indelible print on Islam as a whole and in particular on Sufism. It finds an expression in the well-known saying of the Prophet: 'Do for this world as if thou wert to live a thousand years and for the next as if thou wert to die to-morrow'. On the one hand it enjoins the perfection—the patient thoroughness we might say—incumbent upon man as representative of God on earth; and on the other hand it demands that he shall be ready to leave this world at a moment's notice. Both injunctions are with a view to nothing but the Will of Heaven; and in the light of the second it is clear that the first must be carried out in a spirit of detachment, for readiness to leave precludes involvement. The Prophet was thus able to say also, without any inconsistency: 'Be in this world as a stranger or as a passer-by'.

His other-worldliness needs emphasising in that it has been so much overlooked in the West, largely because his historically striking aspect of earthly plenitude—sometimes totally

[1] Muhammad was not only shepherd, merchant, hermit, exile, soldier, law-giver and prophet-priest-king; he was also an orphan (but with a remarkably loving grandfather and uncle), for many years the husband of one wife much older than himself, a many times bereaved father, a widower, and finally the husband of many wives, some much younger than himself.

misunderstood as 'worldliness'—has been thought to contradict it, whereas the two aspects are, as we have seen, complementary and interdependent. It is significant that in holding out the Prophet as an example to be followed the Qur'ān dwells above all on 'the ebb of the wave': *Verily in the Messenger of God is a fair example for those of you that set their hopes on God and the Last Day, and remember God much.*[2] This mention of *the Last Day* is a reminder that like the Qur'ān itself the Prophet also is haunted by the Hour; and this hauntedness cannot be dissociated from one of the basic events of his mission, the Night Journey, named also, in view of the main part of it, the Ascent.[3] It was as if his 'readiness to leave' had suddenly overflowed from the highest plane on to every other plane so that, for him, the Hour was briefly anticipated and he was given a foretaste of the Resurrection: from the Rock in Jerusalem, to which he had been miraculously transported from Mecca, he was 'decreated', that is, reabsorbed, body into soul, soul into Spirit, and Spirit into the Divine Presence. This 'reabsorption' traces out the line of the Sufi path[4] and its aspect of 'anticipation' is also significant, for this is one of the basic meanings contained in the word *sābiqūn* which was translated in the last chapter as 'foremost' and which is, as we have seen, one of the Quranic terms for the mystics of Islam. We are reminded in this connection of the saying of the Prophet: 'Die before ye die'. It is true that all mysticisms possess similar formulations and all are anticipations; but although the distinction is a relative one, Sufism, as the last mysticism of this cycle of time, is bound to be especially

[2] XXXIII: 21.

[3] The two great nights of the Islamic year are *Laylat al-Qadr* (the Night of Worth) and *Laylat al-Mi'rāj* (the Night of the Ascent). These are respectively, the night of the Descent of the Qur'ān and the night of the Ascent of the Prophet.

[4] Not, needless to say, in what concerned the body and soul of the Prophet, but as regards the essential, that is the reabsorption of the centre of consciousness.

characterised by sensitivity to the 'pull' of the Hour—an added momentum which is no doubt a part compensation for the unfavourable outward conditions of the age.

The Sufis are also acutely aware that this sensitivity must be combined with active effort in the same direction; and in this as in everything else they are, to use their own phrase, 'the heirs of the Messenger'. If Muhammad is the Prophet of the Hour, this is the passive complement of his more active function as the Prophet of Orientation and Pilgrimage. The Qur'ān mentions him as being especially concerned with orientation;[5] and we can measure the weight of that concern by the depth of the impression that it has made upon his people. To the present day, one of the most immediately striking features of the Islamic community is what might be called 'direction-consciousness'. This spiritual asset, inextricably bound up as it is with the consciousness of being 'for God', is also no doubt a Providential compensation; and it applies in particular to the Sufi who, in addition to being more dedicated and more 'path-minded' than the rest of his community, has not only to pray like them the ritual prayer in the direction of Mecca but has to perform many other rites for which he prefers to face the same way, so that this outward or symbolic 'concentration' may serve as a support for inward concentration.

That the Prophet and his closest Companions should have migrated from Mecca to Medina was a cosmic necessity so that the orientation could take on, already in the apostolic age and therefore as an apostolic precedent, the added intensity of the turning of an exile towards his home. It still retains much of that nostalgia to this day, in the sense that a Muslim—be he Arab or non-Arab—is conscious that his spiritual roots are in Mecca[6]—a consciousness that is regularly sharpened once a

[5] II: 144.

[6] The feeling in question is inextricably bound up with nostalgia for the Prophet; and to turn towards Mecca, the place of his birth and

year in every Islamic community by the setting off and return of pilgrims; and in the five daily ritual prayers each cycle of movements culminates in a prostration which could be described as a pouring out of the soul in the direction of Mecca. It must not be forgotten however that *remembrance of God is greater* (than the ritual prayer),[7] and one of the meanings of this key passage is that turning towards the inner Centre is 'greater' than turning towards the outer centre. The ideal is for the two to be simultaneous, inasmuch as the outward turning was above all instituted for the sake of the inward turning. 'Our performance of the rites of worship is considered strong or weak according to the degree of our remembrance of God while performing them.'[8] This question, that is, the esoteric performance of exoteric rites, will be considered later in more detail. The point to be made here is that for the Sufis the spiritual path is not only the Greater Holy War but also, even more, the 'Greater Prayer' and the 'Greater Pilgrimage'.

The Kaaba (literally 'cube' for such is its shape), the 'House of God' in the centre of Mecca, is a symbol of the Centre of our being. When the exile turns his face in the direction of Mecca he aspires above all, if he is a Sufi, to the inward return, to the reintegration of the fragmented finite individual self into the Infinititude of the Divine Self.

Since man is an exile, a spiritual centre will be more powerfully symbolic of home if it is not immediately accessible. That is no doubt one of the reasons why in Mecca, at the outset of Islam, the prayer was made towards Jerusalem. But if man is primarily an exile by reason of his separate existence from God, he is secondarily so by reason of his fall from Paradise.

of the outset of Islam, is practically speaking (except for the small minority who live in those parts) to turn also towards Medina where he triumphed and died and is buried.

[7] Qur'ān XXIX: 45.

[8] Said by Shaykh al-'Alawī. See the author's *A Sufi Saint of the Twentieth Century* (Allen & Unwin, 1971), p. 97.

Two homecomings have therefore to be made, and it was doubtless on account of man's secondary exile that on the Night Journey the Prophet was first transported 'horizontally' from Mecca to Jerusalem before he made his 'vertical' Ascent, so that his journey might be a more perfect prototype of the path that had to be followed by *the foremost* of his people. Only from the centre of the earthly state, that is, from the degree of human perfection, is it possible to have access to the higher states of being. The first part of the Night Journey is as a demonstration of this truth, according to the symbolism of space but regardless of persons, that is, regardless of the fact that the Prophet is himself a personification of the centre, whether it be named 'Jerusalem' or 'Mecca'.

In him the lost perfection is remanifested. It corresponds to the culmination of the flow of the wave, the point from which the ebb begins. We have already seen that the ideal is 'earthly plenitude' combined with 'readiness to leave' and it is to this perfection, poised between flow and ebb, that the initial aspiration of the mystic must be directed. The Divine Messenger enters and leaves this world by the celestial gate towards which all mysticism is orientated. But the mystic himself, like other men, has entered this world through a gate that is merely cosmic; and to avoid ebbing back through such a gate, his little individual wave of entry must reach the culminating point of the great wave in order that its own relatively feeble current may be overpowered by the great current and drawn along with it.[9] Not that the mystic could ever reach this central point of perfection by his own efforts. But the Prophet himself is always present at this centre, and to those who are not, he has the power to throw out a 'life-line', that is, a chain (*silsilah*) that traces a spiritual lineage back to himself.

[9] This being 'overpowered' is no less than sanctification. As regards salvation, the outward forms of the religion are, to continue our initial image, like consecrated hollows into which the individual wave must flow in order to be 'saved' from ebbing back the way it came.

Every Sufi order (*ṭarīqah*) is descended from the Prophet in this way, and initiation into a *ṭarīqah* means attachment to its particular chain. This confers a virtual centrality, that is, a virtual reintegration into the Primordial State which has then to be made actual.

The great protoype of the Sufi rite of initiation is an event which took place at a crucial moment in the history of Islam about four years before the death of the Prophet when, sitting beneath a tree, he called on those of his Companions who were present to pledge their allegiance to him over and above the pledge they made at their entry into Islam. In some orders this rite of hand-clasping is supplemented,[10] and in some replaced, by other forms of initiation, one of which is particularly suggestive of the chain as a life-line: the Shaykh holds out his rosary to the novice who clasps the other end while the formula of initiation is pronounced.

Attachment to the spiritual chain gives the initiate not only the means of preventing his own ebb back in the direction from which he came, but also the means of advancing along the spiritual path if he is qualified for 'travel'. The pull of the chain infinitely transcends the efforts of the traveller, which are nonetheless necessary to bring it into operation. A holy tradition says: 'If he (My slave) draweth nearer unto Me by a span, I draw nearer unto him by a cubit, and if he draweth nearer unto Me by a cubit, I draw nearer unto him by a fathom; and if he cometh unto Me slowly, I come unto him speedily.'

Needless to say, spatial symbolism is not capable of doing justice to the workings of the *barakah* (spiritual influence). To insist on the path as being precisely a horizontal movement followed by an ascent would be a simplification, for the virtuality which is conferred by attachment to the chain makes it possible to anticipate the second part of the journey already during the first part. Moreover, it is part of the method of

[10] As for example in this already mentioned rite of investiture.

all mysticism to proceed as if the virtual were in fact already actual. Even the novice must aspire to the ascent, though he must remain alertly aware of the shortcomings that for the moment prevent this aspiration from being realised. We must also remember that although the chain traces a historical and therefore 'horizontal' line back the Prophet whose earthly perfection is the sole basis for the ascent, that perfection is brought within the orbit of the disciple in the person of the Shaykh, who is already at the centre, already submerged in the nature of the Prophet and already assimilated.

The prototype of the pact between Master and disciple is mentioned in the Qur'ān as follows:

God was well pleased with the believers when they pledged allegiance unto thee beneath the tree. He knew what was in their hearts and sent down the Spirit of Peace upon them and hath rewarded them with a near victory.[11]

The tree stands for the Tree of Life and indicates the centrality which the initiation virtually confers. The 'near victory' is the actualisation of that centrality. The literal meaning of the text did not come fully to light until two years later when Mecca, the outer centre, opened its gates without any bloodshed to the conquering army of the Prophet. The Qur'ān follows the above passage with reference to other spoils which will be won later, and literally these can be none other than the riches of Persia and more remote lands in the East and also in the West which were shortly to become part of the Islamic Empire. But such is the manner of expression that the deeper meaning shines visibly through the literal one: *Other spoils which ye have not yet been able to achieve but which God encompasseth.*[12] For the Sufis these words refer above all to the Treasures of the Divine Infinitude which only the Infinite Himself has power to encompass.[13]

[11] XLVIII: 18. [12] XLVIII: 21.

[13] This verb immediately evokes the Divine Name *al-Muḥīṭ*, the All-Encompassing, a Name of the Infinite.

That the Divine Promise of victory should extend as far as this supreme finality is already implicit in the opening verb of the earlier passage, *raḍiya*, 'was well pleased'. The verbal noun is *riḍwān*, 'good pleasure', but such a translation is extremely inadequate. To realise this inadequacy we have only to remember that according to the Qur'ān, *the Riḍwān of God is greater* than Paradise.[14] To bring out the meaning more clearly let us consider the word 'reabsorption' which has already been applied to the Night Journey of the Prophet as marking out the spiritual path. Very relevant in this connection is the following passage which dwells on the same universal truth: 'We cannot exist in opposition to Being, nor can we think in opposition to Intelligence; we have no choice but to match our own rhythms with those of the Infinite. When we breathe, one part of the air is assimilated, another part is rejected. The same is true of the reabsorption of universal manifestation; only that remains close to God which conforms to His nature'.[15] This passage reminds us also of the already mentioned Qur'ānic term 'those brought near to God' which, like *Riḍwān*, is only used of the highest Saints. The meaning of *Riḍwān* is no less than God's acceptance of us in the sense of our being assimilated, not rejected. In other words, the supreme aim of Sufism is to be 'breathed in' by God and reabsorbed and therefore not subsequently 'breathed out'.

In connection with *Riḍwān* being greater than Paradise, it must be remembered that this applies to Paradise in a relative sense. But in its highest sense the word Paradise denotes the Unsurpassable, and this is the Paradise of the Essence. On one occasion the Qur'ān suddenly turns as it were aside with the following intimate mystical message; and here the concepts of *Riḍwān* and of Paradise are synonymous in relating to the End of the path, that is, to the Absolute and the Infinite:

[14] IX: 72.

[15] Frithjof Schuon, *In the Tracks of Buddhism* (Allen & Unwin, 1968), pp. 63–4.

O thou soul which are at peace, return unto thy Lord, with gladness that is thine in Him and His in thee.[16] *Enter thou among My slaves. Enter thou My Paradise.*[17] The last words refer to what the Sufis term 'Eternality after extinction',[18] the extinction itself being implicit in the word 'slaves'. We are reminded here of the saying of a Persian Sufi: 'I went in and left myself outside'; for since nothing can be added to the Paradise of the Infinite, only nothing can enter it.

After mentioning the name of a Saint, Muslims add 'May God be well pleased with him (or her)' the mention of *Riḍwān* being as a seal upon sainthood,[19] that is, upon the grace of having been breathed in and assimilated by the Divine Nature. A Messenger on the other hand is a manifestation of that Nature; his being 'sent' does not mean that he has been 'breathed out' in the sense that he would need to be reassimilated. On the contrary, he is there to assimilate souls for the Infinite and the Eternal of which he is as a mysterious presence in the domain of the finite and the temporal. Thus in speaking of the initiatory pact of allegiance which virtually bestows that assimilation, the Qur'ān says: *Verily they who pledge unto thee their allegiance pledge it unto none but God. The Hand of God is above their hands.*[20] It is in virtue of this union or identity that the finite self of the Messenger is forever being as it were overtaken and overwhelmed by the Infinite and made one with It, and this overwhelming is expressed in the verb *ṣallà* which is always used after mentioning the name of the Prophet as it was used in his lifetime; 'May God whelm him in Glory and give him Peace'. The prayer for Peace

[16] That is, with mutual *Riḍwān*.

[17] LXXXIX: 27–30.

[18] *al-Baqā' ba'd al-fanā'*.

[19] The general prayer for the dead, 'May God have Mercy on him (or her)' is intended as a seal upon salvation at the least. As regards what it can mean at the most, it is enough to remember that Mercy is by definition Infinite.

[20] XLVIII: 10.

(*salām*) is added to make harmoniously possible what is logically a contradiction in terms, the Presence of the Infinite in the finite.

To go back once more to the starting point of these considerations, it is in a sense to be expected that the Prophet should offer, by way of complement or concordant reaction to his profound descent into the domain of human life, an initiation which confers no less than a virtual *Riḍwān*. In parallel terms, Islam's deep penetration into the affairs of this world demands that its mysticism shall be correspondingly exalted. The aim and end of Sufism is explicitly the Supreme Station in the most absolute sense that this term can have. Although many Sufi treatises speak of degrees and stations, these are as signposts upon the path. There are no intermediary resting places. 'Is it not face to face with the Truth that our riders dismount?.'[21]

Having been given access to the Divine Messenger through attachment to the spiritual chain and having received from him the virtuality of *Riḍwān*, how is this virtual assimilation or reabsorption to be actualised? One of the means which he offers is the invocation of blessings upon himself according to the already mentioned formula of Glory and Peace. 'An Angel came unto me and said: "God saith: None of thy people invoketh blessing upon thee but I invoke blessings upon him tenfold".'[22] But the Glory which is invoked upon Muhammad cannot be refracted the promised ten times upon the invoker until that invoker has actually realised the central perfection which alone has the capacity to receive the Glory and the strength to endure it. In other words, the name *Muḥammad*, in addition to its reference to the Messenger, can and should mean for the invoker 'the virtual perfection that I

[21] Shaykh Aḥmad al-'Alawī, *Dīwān*, quoted in *A Sufi Saint of the Twentieth Century*, p. 218.

[22] This is only one of many utterances of the Prophet to the same effect.

carry within me', while at the same time this name acts as a shield—or rather a filtre—to protect virtuality from receiving what only actuality can bear. This is one of many examples of the already mentioned possibility of anticipating the second part of the journey before the first has been brought to an end. Most of the spiritual work is a storing up of grace which cannot take effect until the readiness to receive it has been achieved.

Another means of becoming submerged in the nature of the Prophet is to recite his names and the litanies that are associated with them. Yet another, the most direct of all, is to dwell in particular on one of these names, *Dhikru 'Llāh*, the Remembrance of God, and to become like him a personification of all that this name implies.

Chapter 5

The Heart

'To-day[1] Sufism (*taṣawwuf*) is a name without a reality. It was once a reality without a name.' Commenting on this in the following century, Hujwīrī adds: 'In the time of the Companions of the Prophet and their immediate successors this name did not exist, but its reality was in everyone. Now the name exists without the reality.'[2] Similarly, but without being so absolute either in praise or in blame, Ibn Khaldūn remarks that in the first three generations of Islam mysticism was too general to have a special name. But 'when worldliness spread and men tended to become more and more bound up with the ties of this life, those who dedicated themselves to the worship of God were distinguished from the rest by the title of Sufis'.[3]

The word *sūfī* means literally 'woollen' and by extension

[1] In the tenth century, some three hundred years after the Prophet. The speaker is Abū 'l-Ḥasan Fushanjī.

[2] *Kashf al-Mahjūb*, ch. III.

[3] *Muqaddimah*, ch. XI. The final word stands for two words in the original, *ṣūfiyyah* and *mutaṣawwifah*, the English 'Sufi' being commonly used to translate both *ṣūfī* and *mutaṣawwif* (of which the above Arabic terms are the plurals). Strictly speaking, they denote respectively one who is at the end of the path and one who is on the path. There is also a third term, *mustaṣwif*, one who aspires to be a *mutaṣawwif* (see Victor Danner, 'The Necessity for the Rise of the Term Sufi' in *Studies in Comparative Religion* (Spring, 1972)).

'wearer of wool', and there can be little doubt that woollen dress was already associated with spirituality in pre-Islamic times. Otherwise the Prophet would hardly have thought it worth mentioning that Moses was clothed entirely in wool when God spoke to him. Nonetheless, the wearing of wool does not appear to have ever been a general practice among the mystics of Islam. The most likely explanation of the name is that it was first aptly applied to a small group who did wear wool and that it was then indiscriminately extended to all the mystics of the community in order to fill a void; for they had as yet no name, and since they were becoming a more and more distinct class, it was becoming more and more necessary to be able to refer to them. The extremely rapid spread of the name Sufi and its subsequent permanence are no doubt to be explained partly in view of this need and also in virtue of the suitability, in more than one respect, of the term itself. The difficulty which people have always had in explaining it is not the least of its advantages since for the majority Sufism itself, by its very nature, is something of an enigma, and as such it calls for a name that is partially enigmatic. At the same time, its name should have venerable associations and profound implications; and the Arabic root, consisting of the three letters *ṣad–wāw–fā'*, which has the basic meaning of 'wool', has according to the science of letters a secret identity[4] with the root *ṣād–fā'–wāw* which has the basic meaning of 'purity' in the sense of what has been sifted, as grain is sifted from chaff. Moreover this root yields a verbal form which, when written without vowels as is normal in Arabic, is identical to the eye with *ṣūfī* and which means 'he was chosen as an intimate friend', the implication being that the chooser was God, as in the case of *al-Muṣṭafà*, the Elect, the Chosen, one of the names of the Prophet, which is also from this root. The

[4] In virtue of the fact that each letter of the alphabet has a particular numerical value, and the letters of both these roots add up to the same total number.

name given to the mystics of Islam is near enough to these other words to be apt, but remote enough for the mystics to accept it without seeming vainglorious. As often as not, however, they speak of themselves as 'the poor', *al-fuqarā'*, plural of *faqīr*, in Persian *darvīsh*, whence the English 'fakir' and 'dervish'.

The poverty in question is the same as in the Beatitude: 'Blessed are the poor in spirit, for theirs is the Kingdom of Heaven'. But the origin of the Sufi term is the verse of the Qur'ān: *God is the Rich and ye are the poor.*[5] Unlike the Beatitude, it refers to mankind in general, expressing a fact from which none can escape. The Sufis apply the verse to themselves because it is they alone who draw from it, as we shall see, the ultimate conclusions. Indeed, Sufism could almost be defined as an exploitation of the fact in question—the double fact, in what concerns God as well as man. Moreover the name *faqīr* has an operative value in that it serves as a precious reminder; and in ending a letter for example, a Sufi will often precede his name with the words: 'from the poor unto his Lord . . .'

If the Qur'ān does not address the Sufis specifically in the words *Ye are the poor*, it does, as we have seen, refer to the Saints, that is, to the fully realised Sufis, as *the slaves of God* in certain contexts where not only the fact of slavehood (which concerns everyone) but also the full consciousness of it is indicated; and the two concepts of slavehood and poverty are inextricably connected. We have also seen that the Sufis, or rather the best of them, are *the foremost* and *the near*. But of all those Qur'ānic terms which may be said to refer to them and to no one else except *a priori* the Prophets, the most significant as well as the most recurrent is probably the somewhat enigmatic phrase *those who have hearts;* and mention of this

[5] XLVII: 38; and also XXXV: 15:

O men, ye are the poor unto God, and
God—He is the Rich, the Object of all Praise.

has been reserved until now because it is important enough to be the central theme of a chapter. For what indeed is Sufism, subjectively speaking, if not 'heart-wakefulness'?

In speaking of the majority, the Qur'ān says: *It is not the eyes that are blind but the hearts.*[6] This shows—and it would be strange if it were otherwise—that the Quranic perspective agrees with that of the whole ancient world, both of East and of West, in attributing vision to the heart and in using this word to indicate not only the bodily organ of that name but also what this corporeal centre gives access to, namely the centre of the soul, which itself is the gateway to a higher 'heart', namely the Spirit. Thus 'heart' is often to be found as a synonym of 'intellect', not in the sense in which this word is misused today but in the full sense of the Latin *intellectus*, that is, the faculty which perceives the transcendent.

In virtue of being the centre of the body, the heart may be said to transcend the rest of the body, although substantially it consists of the same flesh and blood. In other words, while the body as a whole is 'horizontal' in the sense that it is limited to its own plane of existence, the heart has, in addition, a certain 'verticality' for being the lower end of the 'vertical' axis which passes from the Divinity Itself through the centres of all the degrees of the Universe. If we use the imagery suggested by Jacob's Ladder, which is none other than this axis, the bodily heart will be the lowest rung and the ladder itself will represent the whole hierarchy of centres or 'Hearts'[7] one above the other. This image is all the more adequate for representing each centre as separate and distinct from the others and yet at the same time connected with them. It is in virtue of this interconnection, through which the centres are as it were merged into one, that the bodily heart receives Life from the Divinity (according to Sufi doctrine all Life is

[6] XXII: 46.

[7] For the sake of clarity, this word will be written with a capital letter wherever it denotes a transcendent centre.

Divine) and floods the body with Life. In the opposite direction the bodily heart may serve as a focal point for the concentration of all the powers of the soul in its aspiration towards the Infinite, and examples of this methodic practice are to be found in most forms of mysticism and perhaps in all. It is also in virtue of the same interconnection that 'Heart' may be used to indicate the topmost rung of the ladder, that is, the Infinite Self, as in the following Holy Tradition:[8] 'My earth hath not room for Me, neither hath My Heaven, but the Heart of My believing slave hath room for Me.' Another example is to be found in the poem of the Sufi Ḥallāj which begins: 'I saw my Lord with the Eye of the Heart. I said: "Who art thou?" He answered: "Thou".'

From this last point of view, 'Heart' can be considered as synonymous with 'Spirit', which has a Divine as well as a created aspect; and one of the great symbols of the Spirit is the sun which is the 'heart' of our universe. This brings us back to the significance of the name Sufi. We have seen that the word means 'wearer of wool' and that wool is associated with spirituality. But what is the reason for this association? The answer to this question is clearly to be sought for in the science of symbols and in the knowledge that it gives us of mysterious equivalences; and it emerges, as if by chance, from a remark made by René Guénon[9] about the profound connection between two symbols of the Spirit, namely the tree and the sun (represented here by its metal, gold): 'The fruits of the Tree of Life are the golden apples of the Garden of the Hesperides; the golden fleece of the Argonauts, which was also placed on a tree and guarded by a serpent or a dragon, is another symbol of the immortality which man has to reconquer.'[10] Although he does not mention it, Guénon was

[8] See above, p. 23.

[9] Better known in Egypt as 'Abd al-Wāḥid Yaḥyà. He was, by *ṭarīqah*, a Shādhilī.

[10] *The Symbolism of the Cross*, p. 52.

certainly aware that this second symbol is solar not only on account of the gold but also on account of the fleece. Like the lion, the sheep has always been especially sacred to the sun;[11] and so to wear a woollen garment is to put on the raiment of that 'Heart-wakefulness' which is symbolised by the sunlight and which is a central aspect of all that the Sufi sets out to reconquer. The Quranic term *those who have hearts* has thus a relationship even with the name of Sufism as well as being directly expressive of its essence.

So far we have considered the Heart mainly as a centre which includes all its 'vertical' prolongations. But when the term 'Heart' is used in Sufism (as in other mysticisms) of one particular centre as distinct from others, it normally denotes neither the highest nor the lowest but the next to the lowest, that is, the centre of the soul. In the macrocosm, the Garden of Eden is both centre and summit[12] of the earthly state. Analogously the Heart, which in the microcosm corresponds to the Garden, is both centre and summit of the human individuality. More precisely, the Heart corresponds to the centre of the Garden, the point where grows the Tree of Life and where flows the Fountain of Life. The Heart is in fact nothing other than this Fountain, and their identity is implicit in the Arabic word *'ayn* which has the meaning of both 'eye' and 'spring'. The extreme significance of this penultimate degree in the hierarchy of centres is that it marks the threshold of the Beyond, the point at which the natural ends and the supernatural or transcendent begins. The Heart is *the isthmus* (*barzakh*) which is so often mentioned in the Qur'ān[13] as separating *the two seas* which represent Heaven and earth *the sweet fresh-water sea* being the domain of the Spirit whereas *the brackish salt sea* is the domain of soul and body; and when

[11] Astrologically, the sun is said to be 'in dignity' in the sign of *Leo* and 'in exaltation' in the sign of *Aries*.

[12] As such it is often represented as being on top of a mountain.

[13] As for example XXV: 53.

Moses says: *I will not cease until I reach the meeting-place of the two seas*,[14] he is formulating the initial vow that every mystic must make, implicitly if not explicitly, to reach the lost Centre which alone gives access to transcendent knowledge.

One of the Quranic keys to inner meanings is the verse: *We will show them Our signs on the horizons and in themselves.*[15] This draws our attention to the correspondence between outer phenomena and inner faculties, and in considering what is meant by the Heart it is particularly instructive to consider which of 'the signs on the horizons' is its symbol. We have already seen that as the Centre of our whole being, the Heart is the inward Sun. But it is so only in virtue of its 'conjunction' with the Spirit; in its own right, as centre of the soul and threshold of Heaven, it corresponds to the moon. In a fourteenth-century Sufi commentary[16] on the Qur'ān the sun is interpreted as signifying the Spirit; light is gnosis; day is the Beyond, the transcendent world of direct spiritual perception; and night is this world, the world of ignorance or, at its best, the world of indirect reflected knowledge symbolized by moonlight. The moon transmits indirectly the light of the sun to the darkness of night; and analogously the Heart transmits the light of the Spirit to the darkness of the soul. But it is the moonlight that is indirect; the moon itself, when it shines in the night sky, is looking directly at the sun and is itself not in night but in daylight. This symbolism reveals the transcendence of the Heart and explains what is meant when it is said that the Heart is the faculty of direct spiritual (or intellectual) vision. But in fallen man this faculty is veiled; for to say that when man was compelled to leave the Earthly Paradise he lost contact with the Fountain of Life

[14] XVIII: 60. The Fountain is here replaced by the celestial sea whose waters are the Waters of Life.

[15] XLI: 53.

[16] By 'Abd ar-Razzāq al-Kāshānī, wrongly attributed also to Ibn 'Arabī.

amounts to saying that he no longer had direct access to the Heart. The soul of fallen man is thus comparable to a clouded night; and this brings us to a question of fundamental importance for Sufism: if it be asked what qualification is necessary for entry into a Sufi order, or what is it that impels anyone to seek initiation, the answer will be that the clouds in the night of the soul must be thin enough to allow at least some glimmer of Heart-light to penetrate the gloom. A Shaykh of this century, when asked how it was that would-be novices came to him although his disciples made no attempt to proselytise, replied that they came because they were 'haunted by the thought of God'.[17] In other words, they came because the clouds were not thick enough to keep out the awareness of spiritual reality. We may also reflect, in this context, on the phrase 'to have a presentiment of one's higher states'. This presentiment was mentioned by Guénon as a valid motive for seeking to embark on a spiritual path and as a criterion of qualification for the path. The higher states are the spiritual degrees which are centred in hierarchy, one above the other, along the Axis of the World which is none other than the Tree of Life, the Ray of Light which connects the inward Sun with the inward Moon, the Spirit with the Heart; and the crown of this presentiment is the sense, however remote it may be, of what the same author translated as the 'Supreme Identity'[18]—in other words, a foretaste of the truth expressed in the lines which have just been quoted from Ḥallāj.

The word 'foretaste' enters in here with a view to the Arabic *dhawq* (taste), a term much used by the Sufis following the Prophet to denote the directness of Heart-knowledge as opposed to mind-knowledge. Ghazālī in fact defines Sufism as *dhawq*; and in order to understand how this knowledge which belongs to the summit of the soul and the threshold of

[17] Shaykh Aḥmad al-'Alawī. See *A Sufi Saint of the Twentieth Century*, p. 21.

[18] In Arabic *tawḥīd*, literally 'realisation of Oneness'.

Heaven can have need of a term borrowed from the knowledge which is experienced at the soul's lower boundary, the threshold of the body, it is necessary first to understand the universal law of which this 'need' is a particular application.

When it is said that God is Love, the highest meaning this can have is that the Archetypes of all the positive relationships—conjugal, parental, filial and fraternal—are Indivisibly One in the Infinite Self-Sufficing Perfection of the Divine Essence.[19] A less absolute meaning is that the central relationship, namely the conjugal one on which the others depend and in the background of which they are already present, has its Archetype in the polarisation of the Divine Qualities into Qualities of Majesty and Qualities of Beauty. It results from this Archetype that mutual concord depends on likeness and unlikeness, affinity and complementarity. Both the Majesty and the Beauty are Infinite and Eternal, whence their affinity. But one is Active Perfection and the other is Passive Perfection,[20] whence their complementarity. On earth the human pair have affinity through their vice-regency for God, and they are complementary through being man and woman. The harmony of the universe depends on analogous samenesses and differences not only between individuals but also between worlds. The relationship may be 'horizontal' where both poles are on the same plane as in the examples already given, or it may be 'vertical' as between a higher world and a lower world which is its manifestation or symbol. In this latter case the parental-filial relationship is stressed, but by no means exclusively; the conjugal relationship is always there inasmuch as the Divine Immanence can never be excluded. Thus it is possible to speak of 'the Marriage of Heaven and Earth'; and it is also in virtue of the Divine Immanence, which puts the Lover

[19] The Divine Name which expresses this Self-Sufficiency is *aṣ-Ṣamad*.

[20] Active and Passive Perfection are the Taoist equivalent of the Sufi terms Majesty and Beauty.

virtually on a level with the Beloved, that the Sufi poems addressed to the Divinity under the name of Laylà[21] are love poems in the most central sense. The all-embracing example of the vertical relationship is to be found in the already quoted Holy Tradition 'I was a Hidden Treasure and I wished to be known and so I created the world'. There is nothing in the world which has not its Divine Archetype. But harmony demands also that the world shall be a complement, and complementarity implies invertedness. Thus man, whose Archetype is the Divine Being Itself from which everything derives, is the last of all created things, the finality towards which all creation tends. It is this precedent that causes, on the lowest plane of all, the reflection of an object to be a faithful yet inverted image of the object itself. The mountain whose top appears to be at the bottom of the lake which reflects it is a natural prototype of the Seal of Solomon, the world-wide symbol of the Union of the Active and Passive Perfections and by extension the symbol of all the pairs which are the images of this Union throughout the worlds of the universe.[22]

The perfect balance of the primordial soul depends on the harmonious union of the domains of inner and outer man. If we take the apex of the upper triangle of the Seal of Solomon to represent the Heart's direct experience of Spiritual Truths which are the fruits of the Tree of Life, the down-turned apex of the lower[23] triangle will represent taste in the literal sense, whereas the two interpenetrating bases will represent the indirect mind-knowledge which derives from the two direct experiences. The Seal's message here is that if we want to know

[21] This name of one of the greatest heroines of the Near East has the literal meaning of 'night' and is used by the Sufis to denote the Mystery of the Divine Essence.

[22] See in this connection Abū Bakr Sirāj ad-Dīn, *The Book of Cert ainty* (Samuel Weiser, New York), ch. XIII.

[23] The outer is 'below' the inner.

what Heart-knowledge is like we must consult the senses rather than the mind, at any rate as regards directness. But our symbol also figures the gulf which separates the senses from the Heart: sense-knowledge, being the lowest mode of perception, is the most deeply submerged in space and time and other earthly conditions and is therefore narrower and more fleeting than mind-knowledge, whereas the inner 'taste' escapes from these conditions in virtue of its exaltation and is thus of all experiences the vastest and most enduring.

The Seal of Solomon is a key to the interpretation of many texts which have eluded the comprehension of those who are ignorant of the laws of symbolism, and amongst such texts are the Quranic descriptions of Paradise. It is true that spiritual bliss is often indicated simply by an affirmation that there is no common measure between earthly and heavenly joys, or by such words as *Verily thy Lord shall give and give unto thee and thou shalt be satisfied.*[24] But in descriptive passages, the Qur'ān speaks in terms of the pleasures of the senses, because these direct pleasures are in fact the earthly projections or shadows of the Paradisal archetypes which it is seeking to convey. Having their roots in these archetypes, the sensations have power to recall them, for the 'tether' which attaches the symbol to its reality not only traces the path by which the symbol came into existence but can become, in the opposite direction, a vibrating chord of spiritual remembrance.

These Quranic descriptions, while serving to remind the soul that Paradise is intensely desirable,[25] serve also to

[24] XCIII: 5.

[25] Fallen man, if left to his own resources, is in something of a quandary between mind-knowledge and sense-knowledge: he knows that mind-knowledge is higher than sense-knowledge and that it must be rated accordingly; but he knows also that the lower knowledge has an intensity and directness that the higher knowledge lacks. The doctrine of Heart-knowledge explains everything; but failing this, and failing its prolongation, faith, and the virtues that go with faith, in particular patience at

re-endow life on earth with a lost dimension; and here lies a significant aspect of Sufism, already hinted at in connection with Islam's claim to be a restoration of the primordial religion. It goes without saying that this claim is above all justified—we might even say only justified—in virtue of Islamic mysticism. Every form of mysticism begins with a quest for the 'primordial state', since this state means human perfection which is the only basis for the spiritual ascent. But the perfection envisaged, although essentially always the same, is not always 'primordial' in its details. What distinguishes Islamic mysticism from many others is that it looks for its ideal to man as he was created, that is, to a perfection which would accord with the Earthly Paradise. As an image of the primordial soul, the Seal of Solomon with its two triangles pointing in opposite directions figures an intense extroversion balanced—and dominated—by an intense introversion, the pull of the outer world being balanced by the pull of the Heart. We have already seen how the Prophet of Islam personifies this harmonious resolution of opposites. The 'pull of the Hour' which was mentioned in this connection may be said to coincide with the magnetism of the Heart inasmuch as consciousness of both lies in the Heart. Moreover it is the Hour which actually reintegrates symbols into their archetypes, and one of the functions of Heart-knowledge is to anticipate this reintegration by continually referring outward objects back to the inner realities they symbolise. Typically representative of the primordial religion is one of the best known utterances of the Prophet: 'Perfume and women have been made dear to me, and coolness hath been brought to mine eyes in the prayer'.[26]

what one does not understand and unpretentious trust in Providence, something appears to be wrong; and the soul finds itself at the brink of a dilemma between hypocrisy and sensuality.

[26] 'Coolness of the eyes' is a proverbial Arabic expression signifying intense pleasure. The passive tense is important here; it is as if the Prophet had said: It has been my destiny to love perfume and women and prayer.

An analogous inward outwardness is characteristic of the Message which as Messenger he received and transmitted. Coming at the end of the cycle of time, it holds out to mankind once more the Book of Nature, the Primordial Revelation whose hieroglyphs are man and the animals, the forests and the fields, the mountains, seas and deserts, sun, moon and stars. One of the Qur'ān's most central teachings is: 'Do not look on the things of this world as independent realities, for they are all in fact entirely dependent for their existence on the Hidden Treasure whose Glory they were created to reveal.' In its own words: *The seven heavens and the earth and all that is therein extol Him, nor is there anything which doth not glorify Him with praise; yet ye understand not their glorification.*[27] And one of the 'refrains' of the Qur'ān is to address the visionaries or potential visionaries among men and bid them meditate on these or those wonders of creation as 'signs'.

This outwardness for the sake of inwardness which characterises Sufism[28] can be figured by a line joining the two apexes of the Seal of Solomon. The faculty of direct outward perception must be connected with the faculty of direct inward perception, and this connection is the already mentioned 'chord of spiritual remembrance' which must be made to vibrate in order that the inward faculty may be awakened and that the 'glorification' may be 'understood'; and beyond that faculty, represented by the upper apex, the 'chord' may be prolonged indefinitely, for the vibration does not stop short at the threshold of Heaven but is aimed at the Infinite. We are here once again at the very centre of our theme, for Sufism is the doctrine and method of this aim, nor is the vibration anything other than a variant of the ebbing wave which

[27] XVII: 44.

[28] This distinction, like many others made throughout this book, is relative and must not be exaggerated. It is a question of accent—as if each mysticism pronounced the same formula with a different intonation and different stresses.

was our initial image. We may take up once more at this point the question 'What is it that ebbs?', for the answer already given, that it is the centre of consciousness that ebbs, will now be clearer in the light of what has been said about the Heart, which always denotes the centre but which, because subjectively this centre is not stationary, may refer to the inward Moon or to the inward Sun or beyond this even to the Essence Itself.

Since everyone has always a centre of consciousness, everyone may be said to have a 'heart'. But the Sufis use the term on principle in a transcendent sense to denote a centre of consciousness which corresponds at least to the inward Moon.

This principle has its roots in the Prophet's definition of *iḥsān* (excellence) which is directly related to Heart-knowledge: 'Excellence is that thou shouldst worship God as if thou sawest Him; for it thou seest Him not, yet He seeth thee.'

'As if thou sawest Him.' As if man were still in full possession of his primordial faculties. The whole of one aspect of Sufi method lies in the word *ka'annaka*, 'as if thou . . .'; and this rule of idealism has many applications, some of which we shall see later. But it needs to be combined with the rule of actualism, the rule of 'but in fact'. No one is more acutely conscious of the fall of man than the mystic—so much so that a thing counts for him as positive according to the measure in which it is capable of setting up a vibration towards the Heart and clearing an access to it.

In principle, since *there is nothing which doth not glorify Him with praise*, everything has this capability. *Yet ye understand not their glorification.* It has to be admitted that the symbols which could penetrate the Heart of primordial man are prevented from being fully operative for fallen man by his obstructedness. In other words he cannot react to them powerfully enough to effect the necessary vibration; and if left to his own resources he would be impotent to achieve access to the Heart. The sight of a beautiful landscape, for example, arouses not only wonder and delight but also longing inasmuch as the subject cannot merge with the object; and this longing is no less than a degree of the already mentioned presentiment of one's higher possibilities, a degree of 'remembrance' that in the archetypal world of the Spirit a merging of subject with object actually does take place. But such a presentiment would be, in almost every case, no more than a qualification for the spiritual path. In itself it would be hopelessly outmeasured. It is not for nothing that in most traditions the obstacle to be overcome is represented as a gigantic monster with supernatural powers. Nothing will serve short of a sword that has been forged and tempered in Heaven; but as an auxiliary to such a sword, the presentiment will be a precious strength in the soul; in other words, it needs to be consecrated by some Heaven-sent incantation, above all by the Divine Name itself.

It is important to remember here that *Dhikr Allāh* (Remembrance of God or Invocation of God) is a name of the Prophet, and that according to the Qur'ān this invocation is 'greater' even than the ritual prayer. The word in question could also be translated 'greatest', without the comparison, for both interpretations are linguistically possible; and in the present context it can be affirmed that calling on the Name of God, whether it be accompanied by some other experience or not, is the most positive thing in all the world because it sets up the most powerful vibration towards the Heart. The Prophet said: 'There is a polish for everything that taketh away rust; and the polish of the Heart is the invocation of Allāh.'

We are here anticipating the theme of the chapter on method; but like the unity which it aims at establishing, Sufism is so closely knit that it is impossible to isolate, in altogether separate chapters, the doctrine, the method, and the spiritual and psychic substance to which doctrine and method apply. To continue anticipating for a moment, it may be mentioned that although the invocation of the Supreme Name *Allāh* takes precedence over all the other practices of Sufism, the term *Dhikr Allāh* is also extended to other rites and in particular to the recitation or audition of the Qur'ān which is, as we have seen, of one substance with God; and in the context of causing vibration and of the passage from the outward to the inward, it is relevant to quote what the Revealed Book says of itself in virtue of the power of its own verses in this respect: *It causeth the skins of those that fear their Lord to thrill. Then their skins and their hearts grow pliant* (*or supple*) *unto the remembrance of God.*[29] The Sufis have here all the authority they need for using outward movement, such as the swaying of the body in the sacred dance, as a means to inward concentration.

The words *their hearts grow pliant* or, as it could be rendered, *their hearts soften*, can be glossed 'their Hearts grow less hard'. The barrier in question may be spoken of as hardness of heart or rust on the heart or clouds over the Moon or as a dragon that guards the access to the Fountain of Life. If it were not for this barrier, which is the direct result of the fall of man, there would be no need of religion in the ordinary sense, for Revelation could come directly to each man in his Heart which would then refract the Message to the mind and to the rest of the psychic substance. There would thus be a perpetual flow and ebb between the Self and the self. But as things are, a special Messenger has to be sent that he may transmit to others what his Heart receives. This does not mean however that all other souls are entirely cut off from the inward reception of spiritual light. It means that for so tremendous a descent as the Revelation, the Heart must be fully operative as is the case only with the Prophets and the Saints; but between these and the majority is the minority of mystics—'travellers' for whom by definition the barrier is or has become relatively transparent. They seek, as we have seen, to identify themselves with the Prophet and to ebb as he ebbs in response to the

[29] XXXIX: 23.

Revelation. In other words, it must be for the traveller as if the Revelation has come directly to him, in his Heart; and this *ka'anna*, like all the other 'as ifs' of Sufism, is only possible on the basis of certainty.

What then is certainty? Or what is the difference between certainty and conviction? Conviction is indirect and belongs to the mind, being the result of purely mental processes such as argument. But certainty, being always direct, belongs to 'the apex of the triangle'. As such it can be the result of sensory perception; hearing or touch or sight can give certainty. But in its spiritual sense, when it has for object the Transcendent, certainty is the result of Heart-knowledge. Moreover, failing this knowledge in its fullest sense, those elements which are nearest the Heart at the summit of the soul must also be considered as faculties of direct perception, albeit in a fragmentary way; and through the light which these faculties of intuition receive in virtue of the transparency of the barrier, a soul may claim to be possessed of a faith which is no less than certainty.

Before closing this chapter, and as a preface to the doctrine which like all mystical doctrines presupposes at least a virtual certainty in the soul—otherwise the seed would 'fall on stony ground'—let us consider the three degrees of certainty as Sufism defines them.[30] The Divine Truth is symbolised by the element fire. The three degrees, in ascending order, are the Lore of Certainty (*'ilm al-yaqīn*), the Eye of Certainty (*'ayn al-yaqīn*) and the Truth of Certainty (*ḥaqq al-yaqīn*). The Lore is the certainty that comes from hearing the fire described; the Eye is the certainty that comes from seeing its flames; the Truth is the certainty which comes from being consumed in it. This last degree is the extinction (*fanā'*) of all otherness which alone gives realisation of the Supreme Identity. The second degree is that of Heart-knowledge, for the Eye which sees

[30] *The Book of Certainty*, already mentioned, is based on the doctrine of these three degrees.

is the Heart. As to the Lore, it is a mental understanding which has been raised to the level of certainty by the faculties of intuition which surround the Heart; and it is one of the functions of the doctrine to awaken these faculties and make them operative.

Chapter 6

The Doctrine

All doctrine is related to the mind; but mystical doctrine, which corresponds to the Lore of Certainty, is a summons to the mind to transcend itself. The Divine Name *Allāh* is the synthesis of all truth and therefore the root of all doctrine, and as such it offers certainty to the Heart and to those elements of the soul which are nearest the Heart. But being a synthesis, it cannot in itself meet the needs of the mind; and so, in order that the whole intelligence including the mind may participate in the spiritual path, the Name as it were holds out a hand to the mental faculties, an extension of itself which offers them lore as well as certainty and which, in addition to being a synthesis, has an analytical aspect on which they can work. This extension of Name is the divinely revealed testification (*shahādah*) that there is *no god but God* (*lā ilāha illā 'Llāh*).[1]

No god but God: for the mind it is a formulation of truth; for the will it is an injunction with regard to truth; but for the Heart and its intuitive prolongations of certainty it is a single synthesis, a Name of Truth, belonging as such to the highest category of Divine Names. This synthetic aspect makes itself felt even when the Shahādah is taken in its analytical sense, for the synthesis is always there in the background,

[1] One of the reasons why the Name as an invocation is 'greatest' is that by refusing to address itself to the mind, it compels the centre of consciousness to recede inwards in the direction of the Heart.

ever ready as it were to reabsorb the formulation back into itself. Thus while necessarily inviting analysis, as it must, the Shahādah seems in a sense to defy analysis. It is both open and closed, obvious and enigmatic; and even in its obviousness it is something of a stranger to the mind which it dazzles with its exceeding simplicity and clarity, just as it also dazzles because it reverberates with hidden implications. Very relevant are the following lines about the Divine Essence:

> 'It is Hidden in Its Own
> Outward Manifestation wherein It doth appear
> As Veil after Veil made to cover Its Glory.'[2]

Analogously, the essential meaning of the Shahādah is veiled by its outer meanings. One such veil, as the author of the above lines remarks elsewhere, is the meaning 'none is worshipable but God'; and he adds that this meaning can be a veil so thick as to make it difficult even for a would-be Sufi to see the meaning which lies at the root of all Sufi doctrine.

To understand this deepest meaning it is necessary to bear in mind that each of the Names of the Divine Essence comprises in Itself, like *Allāh*, the totality of Names and does not merely denote a particular Divine Aspect. The Names of the Essence are thus in a sense interchangeable with *Allāh*, and one such Name is *al-Ḥaqq*, Truth, Reality. We can just as well say that there is no truth but the Truth, no reality but the Reality as that there is no god but God. The meaning of all these is identical. Every Muslim is obliged to believe in theory that there is no reality but the Reality, namely God; but it is only the Sufis, and not even all those who are affiliated to Sufi orders, who are prepared to carry this formulation to its ultimate conclusion. The doctrine which is based on that conclusion is termed 'Oneness of Being', for Reality is that which is, as opposed to that which is not; and if God alone is

[2] The Shaykh al-'Alawī, *Dīwān*, quoted in *A Sufi Saint of the Twentieth Century*, p. 220.

Real, God alone *is*, and there is no being but His Being. It will now be apparent why it was said that the doctrine presupposes at least some virtual degree of certainty in the soul, for the mind that is left to itself, unaided by any ray of intellectual intuition, will be in danger of supposing this term to mean that God is the sum of all existing things. But Absolute Oneness excludes not only addition but also division. According to the Islamic doctrine of Unity, the Divine Infinitude is without parts. The Name *Aḥad* (One), for full justice to be done to its meaning, must be translated 'the Indivisible One-and-Only'. The doctrine of Oneness of Being means that what the eye sees and the mind records is an illusion, and that every apparently separate and finite thing is in Truth the Presence of the One Infinite. *Wheresoever ye turn, there is the Face of God. Verily God is the Infinitely Vast, the Infinitely Knowing*, says the Qur'ān;[3] and the Name of Omniscience is added here to the Name of Omnipresence partly as an argument: if the Divinity knows everything, it follows that the Divinity must be everywhere, for in the Absolute Oneness there is no separative polarity between Subject and Object, between knower and known. To be known by God is thus, mysteriously, to be God.

The chapter of the Qur'ān[4] which, except for the opening chapter, is certainly the best known and the most often recited was revealed to give the Prophet the answer to a question that had been put to him about the nature of God. It begins, like many other passages, with an imperative addressed to him: *Say: He, God, is One (Aḥad)—God, the Absolute Plentitude Sufficing-unto-Himself (aṣ-Ṣamad)*. It is no doubt in virtue of this last Name in apposition to *Allāh* and as complement to the Name of Oneness that the chapter is called the Chapter of Sincerity (*Sūrat al-Ikhlāṣ*). For sincerity implies an unreserved assent, and for this to be achieved, the soul needs to be made aware that the oneness in question is not a desert but a

[3] II: 115. [4] CXII.

totality, that the One-and-Only is the One-and-All, and that if the Indivisible Solitude excludes everything other than Itself, this is because Everything is already there.

For the mind alone and unaided it is impossible to resolve into Oneness the duality of Creator and creation. The already quoted Moroccan Shaykh, al-'Arabī ad-Darqāwī,[5] tells us in his letters how one day, when he was absorbed in the invocation, a persistent inward voice kept repeating to him the verse of the Qur'ān *He is the First and the Last and the Outward and the Inward:*[6] To begin with he paid no attention and continued his own repetition of the Name. 'But finally'—to quote his words—'since it would not leave me in peace, I answered it: "As to His saying that He is the First and the Last and the Inward, I understand it; but as to His saying that He is the Outward, I do not understand it, for we see nothing outward but created things." Then the voice said: "If by His words *and the Outward* anything other than the outward that we see were meant, that would be inward and not outward; but I tell thee *and the Outward.*" And I realised that there is no being but God nor anything in the worlds of the universe save Him Alone, praise and thanks be to God!'[7] To be remembered also in this connection is the saying of the Prophet: 'Thou art the Outward, and there is naught that covereth Thee.' The mind can understand that just as the Names the First and the Last and the Inward exclude the possibility of there being anything before or after God or more inward than God, so His Name the Outward excludes the possibility of there being anything more outward than Him. Similarly, with regard to the saying of the Prophet in connection with the process of creation 'God was, and there was naught with Him' and the Sufi commentary on this, 'He is now even as He was', every sound mind can see that from the point of view of

[5] p. 21, note 6. [6] LVII: 2.

[7] *ar-Rasā'il ad-Darqawiyyah*, no. 12 (See *Letters of a Sufi Master*, p. 8).

orthodoxy this commentary constitutes an overwhelming 'proof' of the Oneness of Being because it demonstrates, as with a lightning flash of clarity, that this doctrine can only be denied on pain of the heresy of implying that God is subject to change. But the mind cannot understand *how* Being can be One any more than it can understand *how* God can be the Outward as well as the Inward; and in accepting these truths theoretically it brings itself to the extreme limit of its own domain. We are here at the parting of the ways: the exoterist will involuntarily recoil, reminding himself and others that to dabble in theological speculation is strongly discouraged; but the virtual mystic will recognise at once that what lies before him is something other than the domain of dogmatic theology, and far from drawing back he will seek to escape from the apparently firm ground of his purely mental standpoint at the risk of being out of his depth.

'Relax the mind and learn to swim', said the Shaykh 'Alī al-Jamal, the Master of the Shaykh ad-Darqāwī, with regard to the state of perplexity. In other words, let go of your mind so that your soul, now out of its depth, may experience the spontaneous stirrings of intuition, just as a body out of its depth in water may experience the spontaneous stirring of its limbs in the movements of swimming, provided that there is no 'straw' to clutch at. Thus the Shaykh ad-Darqāwī himself says, leading up to the above quotation from his Shaykh: 'If thou art in a state of perplexity (*ḥayrah*), hasten not to cling to anything, lest thou close the door of necessity with thine own hand, because for thee this state taketh the place of the Supreme Name.'[8] In other words, an extremity of need is a door held

[8] See *Letters of a Sufi Master*, p. 11. Titus Burchkardt, the translator, gives the following note on the word *ḥayrah*: 'Dismay or perplexity in the face of a situation apparently without issue, or in the face of truths which cannot rationally be reconciled—a mental crisis, when the mind comes up against its own limit. If we understand *ḥayrah* on the mental plane, the advice given here by the Shaykh ad-Darqāwī is reminiscent of

open for the Divinity through which He will enter in response, just as He has bound Himself to respond to invocation[9] which is itself just such an open door; and in respect of invocation, the Supreme Name *Allāh* is, as we have seen, the 'greatest'. The Shaykh ad-Darqāwī is here stressing the alchemical power of spiritual poverty (*faqr*) as a vacuum which demands to be filled; and perplexity is a mode of *faqr*, for it is nothing other than an imperative need—the need to be enlightened.

The study of the doctrine brings the mind to its own upper boundary across which, between it and the Heart, lies the domain of intellectual intuition, or of perplexity, as the case may be. Every mystical doctrine contains aphoristic formulations which can galvanise the soul into transcending the mind and crossing this boundary. But the purpose of the main body of the doctrine is to convey to the mind as much as can be mentally understood so that reason, imagination and the other faculties may be penetrated by the truth, each after its own fashion. For the spiritual path is an offering; it is ultimately an offering of the individual self in exchange for the Supreme Self. But the offering must be acceptable, and the Infinite cannot be expected to accept anything less than a totality. The offering must be all that the offerer has to offer, that is, it must be sincere. The Shaykh ad-Darqāwī was once asked by an exoteric authority why he used a rosary, the implication being that the Prophet had not used one, and that therefore there could be no justification for such a practice. He replied that he did so in order that even his hand might take part in the remembrance of God.

the Zen method of the *koan*, that is, of persistent meditation on certain paradoxes in order to provoke a mental crisis, an utter perplexity, which may open out into supra-rational intuition.' The word *ḥayrah* is closely related to *taḥayyur* which has the purely positive sense of 'wonderment', 'marvelling', as in the saying of the Prophet: 'Lord increase me in marvelling at Thee'.

[9] *I answer the invocation of the invoker when he invoketh me* (Qur'an II: 186).

An example of doctrinal formulation which the mind can assimilate is the Sufi doctrine of the five Divine Presences. This exposition of the Oneness of Being allows for appearances, deceptive though they are, by representing the Truth as a circle of Infinite radiation. One Being means, needless to say, One Presence; but this Presence is both the Outward and the Inward which makes it possible to speak of two Presences, namely, this world and the next; and since the Outward is a Name of the One Divinity, it cannot be isolated and cut off from the other Names, but must partake of the Qualities they denote, amongst which is Inwardness. This world must therefore have an inward as well as an outward aspect, a domain of souls as well as a domain of bodies, just as conversely within the next world the Unmanifested Creator has His outer aspect in the Heavens which are the domain of the Spirit. It is thus in the nature of things to speak of four Presences, beyond which is the Divine Essence Itself, the All-Penetrating All-Embracing Presence of Absolute Oneness.

The *Shahādah* not only corroborates this doctrine by telling us that insofar as anything is real it is divine, that there is no reality but Reality. It also, in its verbal sequence, traces out the five-fold hierarchy. 'In the formula *lā ilāha illā 'Llāh* (no god but God) each of the four words denotes a degree, and the final *hā'* of the Name *Allāh* symbolises the Self (*Huwa*[10]).'[11] This may be commented by saying, from the point of view of the spiritual path, that the first word is as the light of truth cast upon the material world to counterbalance the illusion 'here is reality at its greatest' and to be for the soul as a signpost 'not in this direction'. The second word corresponds to the world of souls which is, precisely, the dangerpoint as regards idolatry. The Qur'ān continually refers to *those who make gods*

[10] Literally 'He', a Name of the Essence.

[11] Frithjof Schuon, *Dimensions of Islam*, p. 147, but for a full exposition of this doctrine see pp. 142–58, i.e. the final chapter, which is entitled 'The Five Divine Presences'.

of their passions; but this usurpation is only possible because the soul is virtually divine. The second word of the *Shahādah* denotes a potential divinity which is placed between two closed doors, one locked and the other unlocked, that is, between an absolute 'no' on the one hand and on the other a conditional 'no' (literally 'if not') which amounts to a conditional 'yes', namely the third word, which stands for the Spirit; and the Spirit and the Angels, which constitute this third Presence, do in fact mediate on behalf of the soul like a 'but' or an 'except'. The word *illā* is as a sigh of relief, an escape from the prison of coagulated forms, and it points the way to the final solution of the fourth word which stands for the two highest Presences. The *Shahādah* is thus as an amulet or talisman of guidance, for it bars the soul from error while being itself, in the flow of its words, a compulsive motion from the predicament of mere virtuality to the Peace of Actuality.

Another example of doctrinal formulation which is immensely helpful to the mind is to be found in the Sufi 'Abd al-Karīm al-Jīlī's[12] use of the image of water and ice to represent Creator and creation in their apparent difference and secret identity. The image is all the truer in that the frozen crystallisation appears to be far more substantial than unfrozen water; and yet when a large piece of ice melts the result is a surprisingly small quantity of water. Analogously the lower worlds, for all their seeming reality, depend for their existence upon a relatively unample Presence[13] compared with that which confers on the Paradises their everlasting bliss; yet here again, everlastingness is not Eternity, nor are the joys of these

[12] In his treatise *al-Insān al-Kāmil* (ch. VII) and in his poem *al-'Ayniyyah.*

[13] Nor is the Presence uniform within one world. In the material world, for example the great symbols or signs of God and of His Qualities, whether they be in the animal, vegetable or mineral world, are what they are in virtue of an outstanding concentration of Divine Presence.

Paradises more than shadows of the Absolute Beatitude of the Supreme Paradise.

The fiveness of the Divine Presence does not contradict its Oneness, that is, the Oneness of Being, for it is always the Same Presence. Nonetheless, from the point of view of Absolute Reality, the fiveness is an illusion since from that point of view the hierarchy has 'already' been folded up, *like the rolling up of a written scroll*,[14] the ice has 'already' melted. The Shahādah expresses both points of view, the relative and the Absolute, in its very substance. Its letters are crystallised into words which correspond, as we have seen, to the different degrees of the hierarchy. But if the words be melted down to the letters they consist of, we find that there is nothing amongst them but *alif*, *lām* and *hā'*, and these are the letters of the Supreme Name.

The 'eye of ice', that is, the eye of illusion, can see nothing but ice. Only the Eye of Water can see water. Thus the Qur'ān says: *Their sight overtaketh Him not, but He overtaketh their sight, and He is the All-Pervading-All-Prevailing, the Infinitely Aware.*[15] Here again what is in one sense a Name of Omnipresence (*al-Laṭīf*) is followed by a Name of Omniscience (*al-Khabīr*). In Reality Being and Seeing are One, and they are God's prerogative. The melting of the ice is the withdrawal of all pretension to usurp this prerogative.

If it be asked: 'Since only God can see God, why is it promised that the pure in heart shall see Him?', the answer is that the 'pure in heart' are precisely those in whom the melting has taken place, and who see with the 'Eye of Water'. The subjectivity which fallen man is conscious of results from the impact of the transcendent inner light upon the semi-opaque and thus impure coagulation which is a barrier between that light and the soul. The ego is a gleam which appears to begin at the barrier, whence the illusion of being a separate and

[14] Qur'ān XXI: 104.

[15] VI: 103.

independent unit. Purity is the transparency of meltedness. It reveals subjectivity as being no less than a whole 'vertical' dimension, a Ray which passes through the Heart, infinitely transcending it on the one hand and on the other passing from it unimpeded into the substance of the soul according to the measure in which that substance is, by its nature, capable of receiving it. The Qur'ān speaks of the Saint as *he who was dead and whom We have brought to life, making for him a light whereby he walketh among men.*[16] The death referred to is the melting of the illusory subject; and it is along the stream of new-born subjective consciousness compounded of Life and of Light that the Divine 'overtakes' the human.

In this connection, with regard to the words *He overtaketh their sight*, it should be mentioned that the many-faceted Name which immediately follows, *al-Laṭīf*, is sometimes translated 'the Loving-Kind'. Altogether, it means no less than 'the Gently All-Pervading All-Prevailing Loving-Kind'. Its presence in this context implies that the overtaking in question is an act of love, which is confirmed by the Holy Tradition: 'When I love him (My slave), I am the Hearing wherewith he heareth and the Sight wherewith he seeth.'[17]

These considerations, which are related to the 'flow of the wave', are necessary as a complement to what has already been said about its ebb and about reabsorption. The Divinity not only receives and assimilates but also overtakes and penetrates. The great example of this is the already mentioned case of the Divine Messenger, who is forever being overtaken and overwhelmed by the Supreme Presence; and we have seen that the invocation of blessings on the Prophet is a means of participating in this 'Transfiguration'[18] provided that the necessary maturity has been reached.

[16] VI: 122. [17] To be quoted more fully in the next chapter.

[18] It is by Self-Manifestation (*at-Tajallī*) that the Divinity overtakes and overwhelms. Thus the Arab Christians use the term *at-tajallī* for the Transfiguration which was, in Christ, a miraculously visible overwhelming of the human nature by the Divine Nature.

With regard to the Immanence of the Supreme Presence in the 'other' Presences, the Shaykh al-'Alawī represents the Divinity as saying:

> 'The veil of creation I have made
> As a screen for the Truth, and in creation there lie
> Secrets which suddenly like springs gush forth forth.'[19]

It follows almost analogously from this that although the mind must be satisfied as far as possible, perplexity is always lying as it were in ambush. Nor could it be otherwise, for there is a sequence to be followed: doctrine, understanding, perplexity,[20] enlightenment; the seed, the stalk, the bud, the flower. The tightly closed bud of perplexity (*ḥayrah*) will open, if given the right conditions, into the flower of wonderment (*taḥayyur*) and the essential of these conditions is 'light'. But the possibilities of enlightenment are not limited to such fragmentary intuitions as a novice might expect to receive. As is clear from the Shaykh ad-Darqāwī's remarks about perplexity, what seems to be a closure from the point of view of the perplexed is in fact an open door through which help adequate to the need is bound to come; and the initial help to be hoped for is enlightenment in the form of the Spiritual Master. His is the Sun in which the novice needs to bask. But the 'door of necessity' must be opened to the full; and the necessity in question is compounded on the one hand of the presentiment of the Truth as an imperative end, and on the other of the consciousness of the intervening gulf and our impotence to cross it by one's own resources.

[19] *Dīwān.*

[20] Needless to say, perplexity in this sense is altogether compatible with serenity, for since serenity is essential both to *faqr* (poverty) and *islām* (submission, resignation), nothing that is incompatible with it could be considered as a normal phase of the spiritual path.

Chapter 7

The Method

'Nothing is more pleasing to Me, as a means for My slave to draw near unto Me, than worship which I have made binding upon him; and My slave ceaseth not to draw near unto Me with added devotions of his free will until I love him; and when I love him I am the Hearing wherewith he heareth and the Sight wherewith he seeth and the Hand whereby he graspeth and the Foot whereon he walketh.'[1]

The whole of Sufism—its aspirations, its practice, and in a sense also even its doctrine—is summed up in this Holy Tradition, which is quoted by the Sufis perhaps more often than any other text apart from the Qur'ān. As may be inferred from it, their practices are of two kinds: rites which are binding on all Muslims, and additional voluntary rites. When a novice enters an order, one of the first things he or she has to do is to acquire an extra dimension which will confer a depth and a height on rites which (assuming an Islamic upbringing) have been performed more or less exoterically since childhood. The obligations of Islam, often known as 'the five pillars', are the *Shahādah*, the ritual prayer five times a day, the alms-giving, the fast of the month of *Ramaḍān*, and the pilgrimage to Mecca if circumstances allow, this last obligation being the only one that is conditional.

We have already seen the difference between the *Shahādah* as fathomed by the Sufis and its superficial meaning 'none is

[1] Bukhārī, Riqāq, 37.

worshipable but God'. But this objective difference involves a corresponding subjective difference, for there arises the question: Who is it that can bear witness that there is no god but God, no reality but the Reality? And for the Sufis the answer to this question lies in the Divine Name *ash-Shahīd* (the Witness) which, significantly enough, comes next to *al-Ḥaqq* (the Truth, the Reality) in the most often recited litany of the Names. If God alone *is*, no testimony can be valid except His. It is hypocrisy to affirm the Oneness of Being from a point of view which is itself in contradiction with the truth, and it was no doubt to galvanise his disciples into awareness of this that Ḥallāj uttered his devastating paradox: 'Whoso testifyeth that God is One thereby setteth up another beside Him (namely his own individual self as testifier)'.[2]

The Witness must be, not the self, but the Self, which means that the soul is not competent to voice the Shahādah. All the Sufi Orders are in agreement about this, though they may differ in their methods of bridging the gap between hyprocrisy and sincerity. In some orders, by contrast with the single recitation which is legally sufficient, the novice is made to recite the Shahādah hundreds of thousands of times in order that he learn to bring it out from a deeper point of consciousness; and even then, although he is allowed doctrinal knowledge of the Oneness of Being, he will not be allowed to meditate on that doctrine if he is judged to be intellectually too dormant.

So far only the first part of the Shahādah has been considered. But this first Pillar of Islam is two-fold. The testifier must testify also that Muḥammad is Messenger of God—*Muḥammadun Rasūlu 'Llāh*. The 'traveller' must learn to see in this also an epitome of the spiritual path, of the wave that can take him to the end of his journey. Both testifications end alike. But whereas *lā ilāhā illa 'Llāh* begins with a negative, which signifies the turning of one's back on the world,

[2] *Akhbar al-Ḥallaj*, no. 49.

Muḥammadun Rasūlu 'Llāh[3] begins with the state of human perfection as starting point for the realisation of all that lies beyond. In other words, there is a chasm between this formula and the novice, who is not allowed in some orders to repeat it methodically until the repetition of the first Shahādah has loosened certain constrictions in his soul and brought him to a point of being able to bridge the gap in aspiration and place his subjectivity in the name *Muḥammad.* The repetition of *Muḥammadun Rasūlu 'Llāh* with emphasis on the first word is like the donning of a splendid robe which is far too large but which has the magic power of making its wearer grow out to its dimensions. Meantime the wearer must scarcely admit to himself that he does not fill it; and it is an important part of the spiritual courtesy (*adab*) of the path that he should also see his fellow disciples as wearers of the same robe and reverence them accordingly. This is another instance of *ka'anna* (as if) which is so characteristic of Sufism, and another example of the primordiality of its perspective. The second *Shahādah* can be taken, methodically, as a refusal to admit that the fall of man has ever taken place.[4] But this point of view needs to be combined with an acute consciousness of the results of the fall, that is of one's own shortcomings and if need be those of others, a consciousness which finds its expression in the first two words of the first *Shahādah*, *lā ilāha*, or simply in the negative first word. The two-fold initial Pillar of Islam can thus be taken as a combination of the standpoints of fallen and unfallen man, and the Sufi must always be ready to move from one to the other and back again.

The second Pillar of Islam—to give one more illustration of the difference between the legal and mystical conception of worship—is the ritual prayer together with the ablution

[3] If *Muḥammadun Rasūlu 'Llāh* expresses the ebb of the wave, the corresponding expression of its flow is to be found in the three letters *Alif-Lām-Mīm*—see above p. 26, note 2.

[4] So also can the first Shahādah, needless to say, in its highest sense.

which is an inseparable part of it. All believers would agree that a rite is a symbolic act and that the ablution symbolises the purification of the soul. But it would no doubt be true to say that the generality of believers look on the ablution simply as a rite which confers a degree of purity judged by Heaven to be sufficient for the performance of the prayer—whence the consciousness of being in a state of legal or ritual purity, a consciousness which must not be underestimated for it is by definition a 'state of grace' and therefore open to all manner of blessings. The Sufi necessarily shares this point of view and this consciousness; but beyond this legal state he is concerned with actual purity which he can 'taste' and which has to be made total and permanent; and for him this ablution is above all a means of extending the purity that has already been achieved and of intensifying his consciousness of it with the help of the transparent and luminous element.

The secret identity between the linguistic root from which *ṣūfī* comes and another root which has the basic meaning of 'pure' has already been mentioned; and there can be little doubt that the term *ṣūfī* came to be accepted and established largely because it conjures up the word *ṣāfī* (pure), thus pointing to a quality which is the beginning and end of all mysticism. In fact Bishr al-Ḥāfī,[5] one of the great early Sufis of Baghdad, said expressly in explaining this term: 'The Sufi is he who keeps his Ḥeart pure (*ṣāfī*).' It must be remembered moreover that not only the ritual act but also the element itself is a symbol, which means that it is linked to a chain of archetypes going back to its Divine Origin. In other words, the water must be considered as flowing into this finite world from the next; and according to the Qur'ān, water is one of the symbols of Mercy (which includes purification), and of Life.[6] The quantity used does not enter into the question. A

[5] d. 842.

[6] See the author's 'The Quranic Symbolism of Water' in *Studies in Comparative Religion* (Summer, 1968).

drop of water as well as a lake symbolises the Infinite Beatitude into which Mercy reintegrates; and the water used in the ablution, when consecrated by the aspiration to return, is above all a vehicle of reintegration or, from another angle, of liberation, for water is likewise a symbol of the Living Substance of Reality set free from the ice of finite forms.

The same End, looked at from a different point of view, is 'enacted' in the ritual prayer in which each cycle of movements leads to a prostration followed by a sitting posture. The Sufis interpret these in the light of the Quranic verse *Everyone therein (in the worlds of creation) passeth away; and there remaineth the Face of thy Lord in Its Majesty and Bounty.*[7] The passing away corresponds to the prostration, and the remaining to the seatedness which is the most compact and stable posture of the whole prayer.[8] From this verse are derived two basic Sufi terms *fanā'* (extinction) and *baqā'* (remaining, subsistence, Eternality); it is not as himself but as the Self that one who has been extinguished can be said to subsist.

Of the voluntary rites of Islam as performed by the Sufis, the invocation of the Name *Allāh* has already been mentioned as by far the most important. There might seem to be a certain contradiction between the opening of the Holy Tradition quoted at the outset of this chapter which sets the obligatory above the voluntary and the Quranic affirmation that *dhikr Allāh*, which is voluntary, is *greater* even than the ritual prayer, which is obligatory. But it must be remembered that although what is obligatory serves to confer a spiritual rhythm on the flow of the hours, the time that it actually takes is relatively short. The voluntary has therefore a potential precedence over it by being capable of embracing and penetrating the whole of life, and this is what those who practise

[7] LV: 26–7.

[8] For a fuller treatment of the significance of these movements, see *A Sufi Saint of the Twentieth Century*, pp. 187–90.

methodically the invocation aim at making it do. The meaning of the Holy Tradition is clearly that what is a legal obligation cannot be replaced, at the whim of an individual, by something which is not. Thus the Sufis are in agreement that the invocation of the Name, in itself the most powerful of all rites, is only acceptable to God on the basis of the invoker's having performed what is obligatory. It could not be a legal obligation itself for power necessarily means danger; and by no means every novice is allowed to proceed at once to the invocation of the Supreme Name.

The recitation of the Qur'ān is no doubt the voluntary rite which is most widely spread throughout the Islamic community as a whole. The Sufis may be said to differ from the majority in that when they recite it—or when they listen to it which is ritually equivalent—they do so as a prolongation of *dhikr Allāh*, with no abatement of their aspiration to return to God. The doctrine of the Uncreatedness of the Revealed Book holds out a means of union which is not to be refused. Moreover the soul has need of the Qur'ān as a complement to the Name, being as it is by its very nature what might be called a multiple unity, and its God-given multiplicity demands a certain direct recognition which it is not the Name's function to accord. The following passage will find an echo in every reader of the Qur'ān. But it concerns the Sufis above all, for they alone are fully conscious of the problem it touches on:

> 'The Quran is, like the world, at the same time one and multiple. The world is a multiplicity which disperses and divides; the Quran is a multiplicity which draws together and leads to Unity. The multiplicity of the holy Book—the diversity of its words, sentences, pictures and stories—fills the soul and then absorbs it and imperceptibly transposes it into the climate of serenity and immutability by a sort of divine "cunning". The soul, which is accustomed to the flux of phenomena, yields to this flux without

resistance; it lives in phenomena and is by them divided and dispersed—even more than that, it actually becomes what it thinks and does. The revealed Discourse has the virtue that it accepts this tendency while at the same time reversing the movement thanks to the celestial nature of the content and the language, so that the fishes of the soul swim without distrust and with their habitual rhythm into the divine net.'[9]

The Name and the Book are two poles between which lie a wealth of possibilities of invocation and litany, some being nearer to one pole and some to the other. The recitation of the two Shahādahs, for example and the invocation of the two Names of Mercy are nearer to the Supreme Name, whereas certain long and complex litanies are more comparable to the Qur'ān and as often as not they largely consist of extracts from it. But the Name may be said to have another complement which is very different from the Revealed Book though parallel to it in the sense that it directly recognises the diffuse nature of the soul, and this is the individual prayer when the suppliant speaks directly to the Divinity as to another person, telling him of his difficulties and his needs, for himself and for those near to him, both living and dead, and asking for favours of various kinds—or not, as the case may be, for it is essential that this prayer should be a spontaneous laying bare of the individual, and no two individuals are alike.

In this connection it must be remembered that night is the symbol of the soul, and that even the unclouded shining of the full moon does not change night into day. Whatever faith the soul may be said to possess can only be very relative as compared with the certainty of the Heart, but it can be more or less a prolongation of that certainty. There is a significant passage in the Qur'ān where Abraham asks God to show him how He brings the dead to life. *Hast thou not faith?* is the divine

[9] Frithjof Schuon, *Understanding Islam*, p. 50.

rejoinder. *Yes, but (show me) so that my heart may be at rest*[10] is his answer. These last words could be glossed: So that the certainty in the depth of my being may be left in peace, untroubled by the surface waves of reason and imagination. The answer is accepted and followed by a miracle of vivification, which proves that the soul has a right to certain concessions. It could in fact be said that the purpose of a miracle is to enable the whole soul to partake supernaturally of an 'absolute' certainty which is normally the prerogative of the Heart; but a small part of this effect can be produced through that most natural and human means, the individual prayer—not by any superimposition of faith but by the elimination of obstacles and distractions. This prayer, like the recitation of the Qur'ān, is shared by the whole community and is generally considered as an adjunct to the ritual prayer, which it normally follows, preceded by the words of the Qur'ān: *Your Lord hath said: Call upon Me and I will answer you.*[11] But the majority are not concerned with method, whereas the Sufi Shaykhs insist on this prayer above all for its methodic value, not only as a means of regular communion for the soul but also as a means for it to unburden itself, that is, to unload some of its inevitable cares and anxieties so that it may be, at any rate in its higher reaches, a prolongation of the peace of the Heart rather than a discontinuity. Nor should the gestural value of this prayer be underrated, for the suppliant, head slightly bowed and hands held out with hollowed empty palms upturned, becomes a soul-penetrating incarnation of spiritual poverty.

It may be concluded from what is taught about human perfection—and this has already been touched on in relation to the Messenger—that the primordial soul is a unified multiple harmony suspended as it were between the next world and this world, that is, between the Inward and the Outward, in such a

[10] II: 260. [11] XL: 60.

way that there is a perfect balance between the pull of the inward signs—the Heart and beyond it the Spirit—and the *signs on the horizons*. This balance has moreover a dynamic aspect in that the Heart sends out through the soul a ray of recognition of the outer signs, the great phenomena of nature; and these by the impact they make on the senses, give rise to a vibration which traverses the soul in an inward direction, so that with man, the last created being, the outward movement of creation is reversed and everything flows back as it were through his Heart to its Eternal and Infinite Source. But in the fallen soul, where the attraction of the Heart is more or less imperceptible, the balance is broken and the scales are heavily weighted in favour of the outer world.

To ask how the true balance can be restored is one way of asking 'What is Sufism?' And the first part of the answer is that an inward movement must be set up in the soul to counteract the pull of the outer world so that the lost harmony can be regained. But this movement presupposes the direct guidance of a Master in the fullest sense of the term.

The mention of this most essential aspect of Sufism brings us to a consideration of the two terms, *qabḍ* (contraction) and *basṭ* (expansion) which occur so frequently in the Sufi treatises. The initial effort to establish a deeper centre of consciousness and to set up a movement towards it is one of *qabḍ*; and something of this contraction must be retained in the sense that it must still be there to control its concordant reaction of *basṭ*, not so as to diminish its amplitude but on the contrary to rescue it from being a return to the limitations of mundanity. The growth of the soul to primordial stature is none other than an aspect of this spiritual expansion as the complement of spiritual contraction. The Qur'ān continually makes a connection between the *qabḍ* of sacrifice and the *basṭ* of growth. It is worth noting also that in Arabic the word for promoting growth (*tazkiyah*) has also the meaning of purification, which can scarcely be brought out in translation, though the two ideas are nonetheless intimately connected, for impurity impedes growth; it is because the channels to and from the Heart are blocked that the fallen soul is stunted, at least in some of its elements. The symbolism of pruning, which is also a means of purification, is particularly illustrative of the principle in question, for pruning, like a *qabḍ* of the soul, is a diminishment with a view to an increase which will go far beyond what was there before the sacrifice. *Who will lend unto God a goodly loan that He may double it for him and add thereunto a bountiful reward?*[12] Such texts are basic in all religions.

An obvious example of *qabḍ* is fasting, but it must be remembered that the Islamic fast is broken at sunset. The month of Ramaḍān, together with the voluntary fasts which are an extension of it, is thus assimilated by the Sufis into the general alternation to which their method subjects them, the days of the month being an aspect of their *qabḍ* just as the nights are an aspect of their *basṭ*.

It is always possible—and this is the highest aim of *qabḍ*—that the concordant *basṭ* will be towards the Heart and beyond it. Nor is this higher possibility, which is a pure grace, precluded by the relatively outward *basṭ* which is all that the soul can command but which is itself a symbol of the inward expansion and therefore a potential instrument of releasing it. The two together constitute the balance of the primordial soul in which *qabḍ* is as it were replaced by the transcendent *basṭ*.

Of all the means at the disposal of the Sufis, it is the spiritual retreat, *khalwah* (literally 'solitude') which constitutes the most rigorous *qabḍ*. This is a prolonged contraction which refuses any expansion other than the grace of a transcendent one. After the example of the Prophet, some orders maintain that the retreat should be made in natural surroundings. In other orders it is made under the supervision of a Shaykh in a room set aside for that purpose.

[12] Qur'ān LVII: 11.

The term *jalwah*[12a] is used collectively to express 'expansive' practices which are a complement to *khalwah*, and the most obvious example of *jalwah* is to be found in the sessions of remembrance (*majālis adh-dhikr*), more or less regular meetings at which the brethren of the order meet to chant litanies and invoke the Divine Name together. In many orders a sacred dance is performed at these meetings, often as a prelude to a session of silent invocation. The most celebrated of these dances is the one given by Jalāl ad-Dīn ar-Rūmī (d. 1273) to his order, the *Mawlawī* (in Turkish Mevlevi) *ṭarīqah*, whose members are thus better known to Westerners as 'the whirling dervishes', 'les derviches tourneurs', or some other equivalent. This dance, which constitutes a most ample *basṭ*, begins nonetheless with the initial *qabḍ* of a stately procession for which the dancer crosses his arms over his breast and clasps his shoulders. A singer chants, to the accompaniment of flutes and drums and sometimes of other instruments. Then at a given moment the Shaykh takes up his position for the folded-up figures to file solemnly past him; and each dancer, as he enters the orbit of the Shaykh's presence, begins to unfold his arms and turn his body round, slowly at first but soon more quickly with his arms now stretched out on either side to their full extent, the right palm upwards as receptacle of Heaven and the left palm downwards to transmit Heaven to earth, and so the whirling continues.

This summary account fails to do justice to the complexity of the dance, but it serves to bring out one essential feature which it has in common with the dances of other orders, namely that the body stands for the Axis of the Universe which is none other than the Tree of Life. The dance is thus a rite of centralisation, a foretaste of the lost Centre and therefore of a lost dimension of depth and of height. It is thereby the equivalent of the Name which also, as we have seen, re-

[12a] More correctly *jilwah*, literally 'unveiling' (of a bride), but the vowel change is deliberate to make a phonetic complement to its opposite.

places the centre, and in fact the invocation of the Name, aloud or in silence, usually accompanies the dance which in any case is intended above all to plunge the dancer into a state of concentration upon Allāh.

Instead of 'usually' it would have been no exaggeration to say 'always', for even if the dancer has not consciously the Name *Allāh* on his tongue, he has another Name of the Essence in his breath, and that is *Huwa* (He) which, as the Sufis know, transforms the very act of life into a perpetual invocation. In the Darqāwī order, a Moroccan branch of the great Shādhilī order, the dance is rigorously reduced to the two essential elements, verticality (implying centrality) and breath, everything else being eliminated and these two being stressed by a rhythmic up and down movement of the body together with a rhythmic rise and fall of the breast as the lungs are filled and emptied.

In connection with the regaining of the transcendent dimension which is the immediate consequence of regaining the Centre, and which is symbolised dynamically by these movements and statically, as in other dances, by the axial significance of the body, it may be mentioned that the mysterious identity between the dance and the Name is confirmed by the verse of the Qur'ān; *A good word is as a good tree; its root is firm, its branches are in heaven.*[13] This may be interpreted: an invocation, and above all the Supreme Name which is the best of good words, is not a flat utterance which spreads horizontally outwards in this world to be lost in thin air, but a vertical continuity of repercussions throughout all the states of being. It is this most essential aspect of *dhikr Allāh* which is symbolised by the sacred dance.

Not every order has its dance, but litany is always a characteristic feature of the sessions of remembrance; and in connection with *qabḍ* and *basṭ* it is important to mention a threefold litany which is of such basic importance that it is regularly

[13] XIV: 24.

recited in most of the orders, varying from one to another only in certain unessential details. The first of its three formulae—they are usually repeated a hundred times—is 'I ask forgiveness of God' to which is added, at its final utterance 'The Infinite—there is no God but He, the Living, the Self-Subsistent, and to Him I turn in repentance';[14] and in this connection we may quote a saying of a great Sufi of Egypt, Dhu 'n- Nūn al-Miṣrī (d. 861): 'The repentance of the generality is from sins, whereas repentance of the elect is from distraction (*ghaflah*).'[15] This last word could also be translated 'scattered negligence' which is precisely a mode of the profane expansion to which the *qabḍ* of repentance is, for the Sufi, an antidote. As a complement to this turning away from the world in the direction of the Heart, the second formula of the litany is the already mentioned invocation of blessings on the Prophet, which is virtually an extremity of *basṭ*. In these two formulae together, recited successively twice a day, there lies a powerful discipline of consecration. It is not so difficult to turn one's back on the world for a phase of *qabḍ*—or rather, let it be said that the fact of belonging to a Sufi order means, or should mean, that the difficulty has in a sense been overcome: but it can be very difficult at first to prevent the subsequent relaxation from being no more than a relapse. The invocation of blessings on the Prophet offers the soul a means of expansion and therefore a virtual relaxation which precludes mundanity. Needless to say, it has to become spontaneous and sincere in order to be an operative *basṭ*. The resistance of the soul in this respect, according to how much of it retains a nostalgia for its former habits, is often surprising to the novice and always instructive.

[14] As regards these last four words—one word in Arabic—it is worth mentioning that repentance, in the Islamic conception of it, is essentially a turning towards God, an image of His turning towards man. In English we normally say that God relents and man repents, but in Arabic exactly the same word is used for both turnings.

[15] Qushayrī, *Risālah*.

It is the state of expansion not that of contraction which is the gauge of spiritual maturity, for no virtue can be said to have been definitely acquired if it recedes when *qabḍ* recedes, nor has a fault been eradicated if it reappears when the pressure of *qabḍ* has been taken off. But more precisely, since *basṭ* has two aspects which the Sufis term drunkenness[16] (*sukr*) and sobriety (*ṣaḥw*), it is the more prevalent state, namely sobriety, which is the true criterion of what has been spiritually achieved. It is to be expected that the soul will be in what might be called a state of sober *basṭ* for by far the greater part of each day.[17] Nonetheless, it is normal that the grace of drunkenness should leave each time its mark, and in fact some Shaykhs describe the Supreme Station as the state of being inwardly drunk and outwardly sober.[18]

The third and last formula of the litany takes *qabḍ* and *basṭ* back to their transcendent archetypes which are respectively *fanā'*[19] (extinction) and *baqā'* (subsistence). The first part, 'There is no god but God, Alone, no sharer', is an extinction.

[16] Owing to the frequent mention of wine in Sufi poetry, it is perhaps worth mentioning here that the only wine that the Sufis allow themselves is that which the Qur'ān allows, namely the wine of Paradise. It is extremely unlikely for example that earthly wine ever crossed the lips of 'Umar ibn al-Fāriḍ (d. 1236), the greatest of Arab Sufi poets and the author of the famous *Khamriyyah* (Winesong) which begins:

> 'We have drunk to the remembrance of the Belovèd a wine
> wherewith we were made drunk before the vine was created.'

[17] Of the two blessings invoked on the Messenger, it is that of Peace which corresponds to sobriety, whereas that of being whelmed in Glory corresponds to drunkenness.

[18] See for example *A Sufi Saint of the Twentieth Century*, p. 168. The Shaykh al-'Alawī uses here the term 'uprootedness' (*iṣṭilām*) more or less as an equivalent of drunkenness.

[19] It must be remembered however that whereas *qabḍ* is merely an approach, *fanā'* is the actual passage through 'the eye of the needle' and therefore cannot be altogether dissociated from its immediate result of *basṭ* and perhaps also of *sukr* (drunkenness).

The second part, 'His is the Kingdom and His this Praise, and He is Infinite in Power' is an expression of the Divine Plentitude—for *baqā'* is at the level of Absolute Reality which excludes all being other than His Being. The already quoted saying 'I went in and left myself outside' could be paraphrased: 'Leaving myself outside (*fanā'*) I went in and found none but myself (*baqā'*)'. We may quote also the lines of Shustari:[20]

> After extinction I came out and I
> Eternal now am, though not as I,
> Yet who am I, O I, but I?

The last formula of the litany is an expression of truth and the subjective counterpart of truth is knowledge. Analogously, in relation to the first and second formulae, instead of *qabḍ* and *basṭ* we may use the terms 'fear' and 'love'; and this brings out even more clearly the basic importance of this litany as an epitome of Sufism which is often said to consist of fear (*makhāfah*), love (*maḥabbah*), and knowledge (*ma'rifah*), inasmuch as these three standpoints comprise between them the whole of man's subjective obligation towards God. Nor is there anything permissible for man with regard to God which they do not comprise.

Meditation (*fikr*) which is an essential aspect of the spiritual path as an accompaniment to *dhikr*, is based on these three standpoints, each of which has two aspects. For example, fear implies danger. One solution is flight. *Flee unto God*[21] says the Qur'ān, and *There is no refuge from God except in Him*[22] which recalls the Holy Tradition: '*Lā ilāha illā 'Llāh* is My fortress, and whoso entereth My fortress is safe from Mine anger.' But danger is also a motive for attack and this standpoint, which is that of the Greater Holy War, has already been touched on.

Both aspects of fear are related to duty and therefore to will-power. 'Human nature comprises three planes: the plane

[20] An Andalusian Sufi (d. 1269). [21] LI: 50. [22] IX: 118.

of the will, the plane of love and the plane of knowledge; each plane is polarised into two complementary modes which appear, respectively, as renunciation and action, peace and fervour, discernment and union.'[23] The third plane transcends man as such, except insofar as it offers him a theme for meditation. 'The two stations or degrees of knowledge could be respectively characterised by the following formulae: "To know only That which is: God"; "To be only That which knows: the Self".'[24]

For the Sufi the great source of meditation is the Qur'ān itself; and with special reference to Sufism the author of the above passages quotes elsewhere[25] Quranic verses to illustrate the profound connection between *dhikr* and *fikr*, that is, between the act of invoking and the different modes of conformity to it which are to be induced into the soul by meditation: *Are not hearts at peace in the remembrance of God?*[26] *Call upon Him in fear and in eager desire;*[27] *Call upon God in humility and in secret.*[28]

The word 'fear' can be taken here to include both its modes, and this station has already been illustrated from other verses. The two modes of love are 'peace' and 'eager desire',[29]

[23] Frithjof Schuon, *Stations of Wisdom* (Perennial Books), p. 148.

[24] Ibid., p. 153. I know of no writing on meditation which can compare with the final chapter of this book unless it be the closing pages of another book by the same author where the six stations of wisdom are defined as antidotes to the six 'great troubles of the soul' (see *Spiritual Perspectives and Human Facts* (Perennial Books, 1970) p. 211).

[25] In an unpublished text.

[26] XIII: 28. [27] VII: 56. [28] VII: 55.

[29] Peace implies the possession of all that one loves. The realism of this standpoint, like that of the other already given examples of the methodic *ka'anna* (as if) of Sufism, lies in the deceptiveness of appearances. In reality the absence of the Beloved is pure illusion, as was expressed by the Moroccan Sufi poet Muḥammad al-Ḥarrāq (a spiritual grandson of the great Shaykh ad-Darqāwī) in the following lines:

Seekest thou Laylà, when she in thee is manifest?

whereas the last verse affirms the two stations of knowledge as bases for the invocation. The truest humility, as enacted in the prostration of the ritual prayer, is no less than *fanā'*, extinction. As to secrecy, it is a question of 'Let not the left hand know what the right hand doeth'. The 'left hand' in this case is the human ego which is excluded from participating in this profoundest of all invocations where the Self is the Invoker as well as the Invoked.

The Qur'ān continually stresses the importance of meditation, as do also the sayings of the Prophet; and in fact *dhikr* and *fikr* may be said to have a function in the spiritual life which is as vital as that of the blood and the veins in the life of the body. Without *fikr*, *dhikr* would be largely inoperative; without *dhikr*, *fikr* would serve no purpose. Meditation predisposes the soul to receive the invocation by opening up channels along which it may flow. It is a question of overcoming all those habits and reactions which are strictly speaking unnatural but which have become 'second nature'. As the above quoted author remarks in another unpublished text on Sufism: 'The result of the persevering practice of comprehension—by meditation—is the inward transformation of the imagination or the subconscious, the acquisition of reflexes that conform to spiritual reality. It is all very well for the intelligence to affirm metaphysical or eschatological truths; the imagination—or subconscious—nonetheless continues to believe firmly in this world, not in God or the next world; every man is *a priori* hypocritical. The way is precisely the passage from natural hypocrisy to spiritual sincerity.'

Thou countest her other, yet other than thee she is not.

(Bughyat al-Mushtāq, p. 170, Bulaq, 1881; with regard to Laylà see above, p. 54, note 21)

Nor has the other standpoint of love, that of 'eager desire', merely the relative realism of corresponding to a lack that is actually experienced even though it be illusory. This standpoint is above all realist in virtue of the Object of desire, *The Infinitely Precious* (*al-'Azīz*) in whose Eternal Present eagerness can never grow old.

This last word is the key to the understanding of the whole chapter. In defining the spiritual ideal, the Qur'ān uses more than once the phrase *sincere unto Him in religion* which means, with regard to the Object in question, total absence of reserve and total assent.

The practices of Sufism need to be varied in order to meet the variety and complexity of the human soul, whose every element must be impregnated with sincerity in both its aspects. *Riḍwān*, Acceptance, is mutual;[30] and sincerity is nothing other than the human *riḍà*[31] without which there can be no Divine Acceptance.

[30] See above, p. 42, note 16.

[31] This is the term normally used to express the human reflection and complement of *Riḍwān*.

Chapter 8

The Exclusiveness of Sufism

Sufism is central, exalted, profound and mysterious; it is inexorable, exacting, powerful, dangerous, aloof—and necessary. This last aspect has to do with its inclusiveness, which will be touched on in the next chapter; the other attributes are aspects of its exclusiveness.

The first four could be summed up by the word 'sacred'. In excluding the profane, as the sacred does by definition, Sufism does not exclude only atheism and agnosticism but also an exoterism which claims to be self-sufficient and to comprise within its narrow compass all that is required of man by way of response to the Divine Revelation. Religion in itself cannot be called profane in any of its aspects but the majority of its adherents, at any rate in later times, form collectively a domain of profanity in which there is a tendency to take everything at its face-value, a domain as it were of two dimensions only. Profanity is a flat outwardness. Sufism's dismissal of it is expressed in the words of the Qur'ān: *Say* Allāh, *then leave them to their idle talk.*[1] The Name *Allāh* is, as we have seen, the *good word* which the Qur'ān likens to a

[1] VI: 91.

good tree. Idle or profane talk, that is, flat outward talk, is the *bad word* which the Qur'ān likens to a *bad tree sprawling uprooted across the ground for lack of firm foundation*.[2]

Enough has already been said to make it clear that Sufism does not exclude the outward as such, nor indeed could it, given that *the Outward* is one of the Divine Names. But in Reality the Outward is One with the Inward. For the Sufi all outwardness must therefore be related to the inward, which is another way of saying that for him this world is the world of symbols. What Sufism excludes is the 'independent' outwardness of profanity in which the ego gives its attention to the things of this world entirely for their own sakes. But methodically, since such outwardness has become 'second nature' to man, it may be necessary to restore the balance by temporally excluding all outwardness in so far as may be possible. It was from this point of view that Ḥātim al-Aṣamm[3] said: 'Every morning Satan saith unto me: What wilt thou eat and what wilt thou put on and where wilt thou dwell? And I say unto him: I will eat death and put on my shroud and dwell in the tomb.'[4]

Sufism has the right to be inexorable because it is based on certainties, not on opinions. It has the obligation to be inexorable because mysticism is the sole repository of Truth in the fullest sense, being concerned above all with the Absolute, the Infinite and the Eternal; and 'If the salt have lost his savour, wherewith shall it be salted?' Without mysticism, Reality would have no voice in the world. There would be no record of the true hierarchy, and no witness that it is continually being violated.

Sufism has the right and the obligation to be inexorable not only objectively as regards declaring that first things are

[2] XIV: 26.

[3] A ninth-century Sufi, known as 'the deaf' (*al-aṣamm*) because on one occasion, in order to avoid entering into conversation with someone, he had pretended to be deaf.

[4] Qushayrī, *Risālah*.

first but also subjectively as regards putting them first—whence its exactingness.

'Knowledge only saves us on condition that it enlists all that we are, only when it is a way and when it works and transforms and wounds our nature even as the plough wounds the soil—Metaphysical knowledge is sacred. It is the right of sacred things to require of man all that he is.'[5]

The exclusive aspect of Sufism only concerns those who are qualified to be 'travellers' in the fullest sense. But paradoxically this exclusive aspect is sometimes a means of inclusion. A few of the multitudes of atheists and agnostics in the world are what they are for reasons which cannot be considered as altogether inexcusable. Atheism or agnosticism can be the revolt of a virtual mystic against the limitations of exoterism; for a man may have in himself, undeveloped, the qualifications for following a spiritual path even in the fullest sense and yet at the same time—and this is more than ever possible in the modern world—he may be ignorant of the existence of religion's mystical dimension. His atheism or agnosticism may be based on the false assumption that religion coincides exactly with the outward and shallow conception of it that many of its so-called 'authorities' exclusively profess. There are souls which are prepared to give either everything or nothing. The inexorable exactingness of Sufism has been known to save those who could be saved by no other means: it has saved them from giving nothing by demanding that they shall give everything.

Sufism is powerful because it is no less than the Divine Means of the all-overwhelming triumph of the Absolute. The Prophet said of the *Shahādah*, which is as we have seen, the epitome of Sufi doctrine and method: 'If the seven Heavens and the seven earths were put in one scale, they would be outweighed by *lā ilāha illā 'Llāh* in the other.' But such active

[5] Frithjof Schuon, *Spiritual Perspectives and Human Facts* (Perennial Books, 1970), p. 138.

forces demand a conformity of passive strength in the soul of anyone who brings them into action. In other words, they demand a patience and steadfastness which will prolong their action enough for them to take effect in a domain which is subject to time. Failing these virtues, which are part of the qualification[6] to enter a Sufi order, there can be great danger in the practice of Sufism as in every incongruous alliance of weakness and strength—'children playing with fire' is the proverbial example. It is true in a sense that every believer must become a Sufi sooner or later, if not in this life then in the next; but it is also true that the great majority suffer from disqualifications that only death can dissolve. It would be dangerous for such people to seek to follow the mystic path, but they are seldom tempted to do so. The danger lies in what might be called border-line cases.

The fact that purification marks the end of Sufism means that the soul of the novice is bound to be relatively impure. In particular, a novice is unlikely to have an altogether pure motive for seeking to join a *ṭarīqah:* legitimate aspiration is liable to be alloyed at first, albeit unconsciously, with individual ambition. The *dhikr* itself eventually sifts 'the grain from the chaff'; the aspiration welcomes it, whereas it arouses the antagonism of the elements of impurity; and when the soul has been divided into two camps for the Greater Holy War, it is to be expected that the scales should be heavily weighted against the enemies of the Spirit. If the soul had not the right inclination to begin with, it would normally not come to the point of seeking to enter an order. Nonetheless, it is by no means impossible that an individual should be attracted to Sufism for predominantly wrong reasons.

[6] The 'presentiment of one's higher possibilities' partly coincides with a degree of what is sometimes called the 'sense of Eternity', and it is impossible that this sense should exist in one direction only. Eternity must first have left its imprint on the soul, and the virtues of patience and steadfastness are a necessary part of that imprint.

From what revealed texts and other authoritative formulations tell us about the scales of Divine measurement, particularly as regards those human attitudes which are the most displeasing to the Divinity, it may be concluded that the doctrine of the Oneness of Being, and with it that of the Supreme Identity, could be, in certain cases, an indirect means of damnation. It is much better for the unintellectual believer to reject this doctrine than to let it act as a soporific for his fear of God and take the edge off his exoteric piety, while it involves him at the same time in an inward conflict for which he has not the strength. The intellectual sees the supreme Identity as it were through the veil of *fanā'*, extinction, which imposes on the soul an inexorable ambition-excluding *faqr*, spiritual poverty, for the sense of the transcendent, which the intellectual possesses by definition, necessarily implies the sense of the relative unimportance of all that is untranscendent and individual. But lack of intellectuality, combined with the mental arrogance which in some degree or other is the normal result of a modern education, can produce the phenomenon of an unenlightened soul incapable of admitting even to itself that any mode of knowledge could be beyond its scope; and for such a soul a contact with Sufism and the discovery of its doctrine and its aims could bring about the worst and most incurable form of 'hardness of heart'.

The profane man is conscious of only a small part of his own soul; and since its whole substance has to be discovered, mystical practices often lead first of all to experiences which are not spiritual but only psychic, however strange and even wonderful they may seem;[7] and it may be that some such

[7] This accounts for some of the current illusions about what can be obtained through drugs. Hagiography is rich in records of Saints to whom the first glimmering of spiritual realisation was only granted after long years of sustained effort. The idea that any comparable result could be achieved by taking a pill betrays a disqualifying lack of sense of the sacred—'sense of God', we might say.

experience could lay bare a hitherto unknown egoic nucleus which lack of intellectual discrimination might deem transcendent. The greatest danger is that this point of individual consciousness should be considered as the Supreme Self, and that the whole doctrine, together with the traditionally recorded experiences of the Saints, should be complacently interpreted as a confirmation and a nourishment for this worst of all self-deceptions.

Such dangers can be avoided altogether by obedience to the Spiritual Master—by being, as the Sufis say, 'like a corpse in the hands of the washer of the dead'. But it is also true that the 'traveller' may reach a point where partially or totally, the inward Guide, can replace the outward guide, and a soul of the kind we have been considering will have the tendency to imagine that this point has been reached. There have also been cases where the guided has outstripped the guide, and the novice in question would be likely to hear of this possibility also, and to open wide his ears, although the guide in the fullest sense is by definition he who cannot be outstripped.[8]

Many utterances have come down to us which are typical of Sufism in its exclusive aspect. The following very significant and far-reaching example is from the lips of one of the greatest women Saints of Islam, Rābi'ah al-'Adawiyyah.[9] When her spiritual advice was sought by a man who said he had not sinned for twenty years, she replied: 'Alas, my son, thine existence is a sin wherewith no other sin may be compared.' This utterance comprises in itself all the qualities of exclusiveness. It makes no concessions to ignorance or obtuseness or any other limitation or weakness. In order to achieve[10] the

[8] See Hujwīrī, *Kashf al-Maḥjūb*, pp. 128–9.

[9] For a study of this early Saint (she died in 801) see Margaret Smith, *Rābia the Mystic* (Cambridge University Press)—reprinted 1974.

[10] Not that there can have been any mental deliberation here. The utterance was clearly inspired, which means that its 'purpose' lay in the domain of the Heart.

startling juxtaposition of that which is most innocent—namely existence—with that which is most guilty, or in other words, for the sake of sharpening, with the barb of paradox, her demonstration of the rights of the Absolute, she sacrifices every other point of view. Law and practical theology are thrown to the winds. The same is true of Hallāj's already quoted 'Whoso testifieth that God is One thereby setteth up another beside Him' which could also be translated: 'To say "One God" is to worship two gods.' The paradox here lies in the 'guilt' of what is a legal obligation. Exactly the same rights of the Absolute were demonstrated by Jesus when he said: 'Why callest thou me good?', and by Muḥammad when he said, 'Every son of Adam is food for the fire except for the mark of the prostration.'[11] But in these two apostolic utterances, there is a hierarchy of meanings at different levels in conformity with the inclusive aspect of mysticism as an integral part of religion as a whole, whereas in the other two formulations the highest truth is stripped of all its coverings to be shot naked like an arrow into the heart of the 'traveller'. And if we may follow this image up with a very different one, all possibilities of interpretation at lower levels are excluded lest the drowning man should have straws to clutch at.

Certain aspects of the structure of Islam are eminently favourable to the characteristics which are the theme of this chapter. The clear distinction between the obligatory and the voluntary, which is in a sense parallel to the distinction between *those of the right* and *the foremost*, that is, between salvation and sanctification, implies also a distinction between exoteric and esoteric responsibility. The majority are provided for by a well-defined legal minimum as a gauge of salvation and the responsibility of the jurists and theologians lies in this

[11] The mark made on the forehead by the prostration is the evidence of the supreme innocence of non-existence apart from God, for prostration in its highest sense signifies, as we have seen, *fanā'* (extinction).

domain. The mystics of Islam—and this is no doubt partly why their heritage has retained its height and its depth—are thus exonerated from proselytising and preaching in the ordinary sense and free to adopt, on occasion though not always, a rigidly exclusive standpoint, as much as to say: 'Take Sufism as it most truly and most deeply is, or leave it.

But here again, exclusiveness may be a means of inclusion, for to point out a gulf is in a sense to challenge men to cross it, and for some souls such a challenge can be no less than a vocation. Moreover, generally speaking, the more exalted a standpoint is, the more universal it will be, and it cannot be denied that the spread of Islam in certain places—in India for example[12]—has been partly due to the exaltation of its mysticism.

[12] Prince Dārā Shikoh (d. 1659), the Sufi son of the Mogul Emperor Shāh Jahan, was able to affirm that Sufism and Advaita Vedāntism are essentially the same, with a surface difference of terminology.

Chapter 9

Sufism throughout the Centuries

The advent of a new religion is always a more or less sudden redress. Islam was no exception: but it was different from the other Divine interventions in being the last of the cycle and therefore in coming at a time of greater degeneration; and in particular it differed from the intervention which brought Christianity in that it established not only a spiritual way but also, almost immediately, a theocratic state. The contrast between that state and what had preceded it and continued to surround it was tremendous. The Qur'ān goes so far as to say addressing Muhammad and his Companions: *Ye are the best people that hath been brought forth (as a pattern) for mankind.*[1] The miraculousness of that community is also made clear: on more than one occasion the Qur'ān mentions that it was God who had attuned, or united, the hearts of the believers; and on the height where it had been providentially placed this *best people* was held by force long enough to be indelibly impressed with certain principles. The natural downward course of the cycle which, for that community, had been arrested by the miracle was only allowed to resume its course when Islam had been firmly established;

[1] III: 110.

and the sharpness with which civil discord soon set in may be considered as partly due to a cosmic reaction against an excellence that was as a violation of the nature of the age in which it had been set. The new state continued nonetheless to be governed, after the death of the Prophet, by four successive Saints, and though this could not stop the steady increase of worldliness and consequent troubles, it was a thing of untold significance, unparalleled elsewhere. Moreover the first and fourth of these caliphs, Abū Bakr the Prophet's closest friend and father-in-law, and 'Alī the Prophet's cousin and son-in-law, are counted by the Sufis as being amongst the greatest of their spiritual ancestors.[2]

The Traditions of the Prophet abound in mystical precepts which show that Muhammad was in fact, as the Sufis insist, the first Sufi Shaykh in all but name. 'All the mystic paths are barred except to him who followeth in the footsteps of the Messenger,' said Junayd,[3] and also 'This our lore is anointed with the sayings of the Messenger of God'. To this day, the differences between the various orders are mainly differences of selection, by the founders of the orders, from the wide range of practices offered by the Prophet's own example and recommendation. But this function of Spiritual Master was knit together with his other functions in the unity of his one person; and analogously the community under him, for all the divergence and disparity of individual gifts and tendencies, was united into one whole as it never was to be again.

To say that it formed a spiritual unity is equivalent to

[2] Ibn 'Arabī affirms that sainthood is greater than prophethood because it is eternal, whereas prophethood is a function which has a beginning and an end, but that the sainthood of a Prophet is greater than that of other Saints; and he maintains that Abū Bakr had attained to an intermediary degree of sainthood, between those of the Prophet and the non-prophet. Other Sufis have said as much of 'Alī, and Muhammad himself said: 'I am the City of Knowledge, and 'Alī is its Gate'.

[3] A Sufi who lived for most of the ninth century in Baghdad, where he died in 910. The two quotations are taken from Qushayrī's *Risālah.*

saying that there was a general response to his own inward and upward attraction; and a powerful factor of this mystical bias was without doubt the presence of a greater number of *the foremost* in proportion to the rest of the community than at any other time. *Many amongst the first generations and few amongst the later generations*[4] says the Qur'ān of *the foremost*; and some of these *many* must be ranked as a prolongation of the sanctifying and magnetic presence of the Messenger himself and therefore as an aspect of the Divine intervention, for it cannot be held that men like the first Caliphs and others of the great Companions simply 'happened' to be of that particular generation, any more than that the two St Johns and St Peter—to mention only three—'happened' to be alive at the time of Christ. Moreover, although it would doubtless be an exaggeration to say with Hujwīrī that Sufism (in all but name) was 'in everyone', it could at least be said that the first community as a whole was open to mysticism as it could never be once certain barriers of exoterism had crystallised. But above all it must be remembered that an apostolic age is by definition an age when the 'Gates of Heaven' have been unlocked. If the night of the Revelation is *better than a thousand months*, it is so because *the Angels and the Spirit descend therein*;[5] and this penetration of the natural by the supernatural, which may be said to continue throughout the mission of the Messenger, is bound to bring certain possibilities within the reach of those who would not normally attain to them. A multitude of souls can be endowed, through the impact of miracles, with a degree of certainty which in other ages is the prerogative only of mystics in the fullest sense; and when sign after sign, both in the Revelation and parallel to it, demonstrates that the Divine Eye is concentrated on the 'chosen people' in question, conditions are exceptionally favourable for a more general attainment of what was soon to become the distinguishing mark of the Sufis alone, namely

[4] LVI: 13–14. [5] XCVII: 4.

iḥsān, 'that thou shouldst worship God as if thou sawest Him, and if thou seest Him not, yet He seeth thee'.

After the death of the Prophet, his spiritual heirs clung to the unity so that his age, the age of excelling oneself, might be prolonged. With his example still fresh in their memories, they had no choice but to apply to themselves the Qur'ān's injunction to him: *Lower thy wing unto those that follow thee.*[6] Without in any way compromising itself, exaltation can cease to be exclusive where there is nothing that needs to be excluded. A Saint will 'lower the wing' for children because they are simple and unprofane, and are themselves ever seeking to 'raise the wing'; and it is inevitable that there should be in a Divine Messenger a transcendent 'parenthood' which has not only a unifying but also a simplifying and 'childifying' effect upon his whole community, regardless of their years.

This must not be taken to mean, however, that the exclusive aspect of Sufism has not also its roots in that age. The Prophet gave some teachings which were not intended to become common knowledge. The following Tradition which is accepted as genuine by Bukhārī, one of the most scrupulously reliable of the traditionists, refers not merely to one such teaching but to a whole category. The speaker is the Companion Abū Hurayrah: 'I have treasured in my memory two stores of knowledge which I had from the Messenger of God. One of them I have made known; but if I divulged the other ye would cut my throat.'[7] Nor does the Qur'ān invariably 'Lower its wing', as is clear from many previous quotations. To add another example, the doctrine of the impermanence of the soul as such is mystical in the most exclusive sense; such words as *everything perisheth but His Face*,[8] though in principle they are for everyone, do in fact exclude the majority by passing over their heads. We have also seen that the Qur'ān is explicit as regards the distinctions it makes in the spiritual hierarchy. But these distinctions, which would certainly

[6] XXVI: 215. [7] '*Ilm*: 42. [8] XXVIII: 88.

have been felt between man and man, were not as yet conformed to by any corresponding outward structure. It was in the nature of things that groups should have been formed spontaneously after the Prophet's death round the more venerable of the Companions, and there can be little doubt that already before he became caliph, 'Alī was the most remarkable of these spiritual centres. But there is no evidence of anything like an order. The only organised brotherhood was that of Islam itself.

If it be asked when was the end of the apostolic age, one answer would be that it ended with the death of the Prophet, which meant the closing of a great door. But another door may be said to have closed with the death of 'Alī. Until then, spiritual authority and temporal power were in fact, as well as in theory, combined in the person of the caliph as they had been in the Prophet. Nor had the spiritual authority been fragmented: the caliph was the legal, theological and mystical head of the community. But after the four 'orthodox caliphs' as they are called, the caliphate became an increasingly dynastic affair, and the caliph retained a spiritual authority which was little more than nominal, whereas its reality began to be divided between the jurisprudents, the theologians and the mystics, each in their own domain.

An outstanding intermediary figure in this period was Ḥasan al-Baṣrī, so named because he spent most of his long life at Basra in Southern Iraq. But he was born in Medina, at the end of the reign of 'Umar, the second caliph, who is said to have given him his blessing and to have foretold great things of him, and as an adolescent, still at Medina, he sat at the feet of 'Alī. It is through this Ḥasan[9] that many of the Sufi orders trace their spiritual descent back to 'Alī, and thus to the Prophet. He is intermediary in the sense that he grew up in the

[9] Not to be confused with Ḥasan, 'Ali's elder son, through whom the Shādhilī Order traces one of its lines of spiritual descent back to the Prophet.

apostolic age, but by the time of his own death at the age of 86 in A.D. 728, the mystics of Islam had become a distinct class.

In virtue of Ḥasan's profound humility and generosity, much of what has come down to us about him is in the form of anecdotes told by him to the credit of others at his own expense. To give an example, Ḥasan's eventual successor, Ḥabīb al-'Ajamī—this last name means 'the Persian'—had considerable difficulty, at any rate as a novice, in pronouncing Arabic. Ḥasan had often prayed with Ḥabīb, and being the master as well as the elder man had led the prayer with his disciple behind him. But on one occasion Ḥabīb had already begun to pray, not realising that Ḥasan was present, so that the normal course would have been for Ḥasan to have taken up his stance behind him, since it is not recommended to perform the ritual prayer alone if there is any alternative. But Ḥabīb's Arabic was so faulty that Ḥasan had doubts as to whether the prayer would be valid, and it is moreover a point of law that if the leader's prayer is invalid, this invalidates that particular prayer for all who have prayed behind him. After a moment's hesitation, Ḥasan prayed the prayer alone. But that night he had a vision in which God reproached him for imagining that in the Divine scale of measurement a purity of intention and a fervour so great as Ḥabīb's could possibly be outweighed by a few mistakes of pronunciation.

In one of his sayings, Ḥasan mentions the possibility of seeing clearly the next life whilst still in this and describes the lasting imprint of this foretaste. He speaks of such visionaries objectively, but it is clear from what he says that he is one of them: 'The onlooker thinketh that they are sick, but no sickness hath smitten that folk. Or, if thou wilt, they are smitten—overwhelmingly smitten by remembrance of the Hereafter.'[10]

He also said: 'He that knoweth God loveth Him, and he

[10] Abū Nu'aym al-Iṣbahānī, *Ḥilyat al-awliyā'*.

that knoweth the world abstaineth from it.'[11] We have here the very quintessence of Sufism, nor is it given to everyone to make such formulations.

Rābi'ah al-'Adawiyyah, also of Basra, was only about 11 years old when Ḥasan died. She therefore belonged in no sense to the first age of Islam, for her whole life was set in the period of steep degeneration which followed it. In a time characterised by so marked a diminishing of the sense of values, it was her vocation—we might almost say mission, for such was her greatness—to incarnate at the highest level, that is, in the domain of the Spirit, the putting of first things first—God before Paradise,[12] the Absolute before the relative. Some of her utterances, like the one quoted at the end of the last chapter, would have been unthinkable in the earlier generations, not for what was expressed but for the manner of expression. The same applies to the utterances of many of her mystic contemporaries. The scruples that made the first Islamic elect so chary of showing themselves to be too different from the generality were now outbalanced by the obligation not to be dragged down by its increasingly 'dead' weight. The initial unity had been lost beyond recall. Dāwud aṭ-Ṭā'ī—disciple and successor of Ḥabīb al-'Ajamī—went so far as to say: 'Fast from this world and make death thy breakfast and flee from men as thou wouldst flee from beasts of prey'[13]

There is however one communal responsibility that Sufism cannot evade, and this is related to its necessity. Sufism is necessary because it is to Islam what the heart is to the body. Like the bodily heart it must be secluded and protected and

[11] Abū Sa'īd al-Kharrāz, *Kitāb aṣ-Ṣidq* (The Book of Truthfulness).

[12] It was in this sense that she would quote *al-jār thumma 'd-dār* (the neighbour, then the house), the Arab version of the world-wide maxim that in choosing a house, it is more important to see who is going to be your neighbour than what the house itself is like.

[13] Qushayrī: *Risālah.*

must remain firm-fixed in the centre; but at the same time it cannot refuse to feed the arteries with life. The relationship between Islamic esoterism and exoterism is thus both complex and delicate, and looked at from the outside it could seem that the Sufis are continually cleaving chasms and building bridges between themselves and the rest of the community. But to divide the mystics of Islam into two categories in this respect would be a most misleading simplification, for all Sufis worthy of the name must be 'hearts' in every sense, after the pattern of their exemplars, of whom the Prophet said: 'The earth shall never be found lacking in forty men of the like of the Friend[14] of the All-Merciful. Through them shall ye be given to drink, and through them shall ye be given to eat.' But the superhuman action of presence referred to here would not be in any way diminished by the human action of 'fleeing from men'. The history of mysticism shows that a recluse may have the most radiant of presences.

The Sufis both early and late are in agreement that one of the very greatest of their number is Junayd.[15] Even his own Shaykh, Sarī as-Saqaṭī, himself among the greatest masters of Sufism, is reported to have said that the rank of his disciple (who was also his nephew) was above his own. It is true that in one sense such a remark is meaningless, for if the word 'great' can be used of Sarī or any other Saint, this means that he or she had attained to extinction in the Divine Essence, that is, in Absolute Greatness. Comparisons can only be made at the level of Divine Manifestation below that of the Supreme and Unmanifested Self. As the Shaykh al-'Alawī remarks: 'The Divine Manifestation varieth in intensity from one person to another. . . . The inward eyes of men are ranged in hierarchy and the secret receptacles are more capacious in some than in others. Even so doth He manifest Himself unto each according to his capacity',[16] and he goes on to speak of

[14] Abraham. [15] See above, p. 101, note 3.
[16] See *A Sufi Saint of the Twentieth Century*, p. 162.

the incomparable magnitude of the inward capacity of the Messenger to receive the Divine Manifestations.[17]

As to knowing this hierarchy of the Saints, all we can do is to accept the opinions of the Saints themselves, and it is they have given Junayd the titles of 'Lord of the Group,'[18] 'Peacock of the Poor', and 'the Shaykh of Shaykhs'.

In addition to those of Junayd's sayings which have already been quoted, the following is particularly related to the title of this book:

'Sufism is that God should make thee die away from thyself and live in Him.' He also said, with regard to the grace of intimacy (*uns*) with God: 'I heard Sarī say: "The slave may reach a point wherein if his face were struck with a sword he would not notice it", and there was something in my heart which assented to this even before the time came when I saw clearly that it was as he had said.'[19]

In connection with Junayd and his contemporaries it is relevant to consider a question concerning spiritual drunkenness (*sukr*) and spiritual sobriety (*ṣaḥw*). These correspond, as we have seen to the two blessings which are invoked upon the Messenger following the Qur'anic injunction, and which are refracted on to the invoker according to his capacity to receive them. This means that no one can be called a Sufi in the fullest sense who does not partake of both. Nonetheless, it is possible to make a distinction between individual Saints according to whether the drunkenness remains entirely inward

[17] It is clearly to these Manifestations that Abū Yazīd al-Bistāmī was referring when he said: 'If a single atom of the Prophet were to manifest itself to creation naught that is beneath the Throne could endure it' (Kalābādhī, *Ta'arruf*, ch. XXIV, in Arberry's translation, *The Doctrine of the Sufis*, p. 54).

[18] The Sufis are often known as 'the Group' (*aṭ-ṭā'ifah*) on account of a verse of the Qur'ān (LXXIII: 20) which refers to a particular group who followed the Prophet in his extreme intensity of worship as opposed to the majority who did not.

[19] Qushayrī, *Risālah*.

or whether, by overflowing, it sometimes eclipses the outward sobriety. Whatever the differences between Ḥasan and Rābi'ah, their spiritual intoxication does not appear to have been expressly manifested outwardly, and the same applies to Junayd in an even more marked degree.[20] But it was not the case with Abū Yazīd al-Bistāmī, for example; and certain of his inspired ejaculations—like those of Hallāj some fifty years later—provoked much hostility against Sufism on the part of the exoteric authorities. It was Abū Yazīd who exclaimed: 'Glory be to Me! How great is My Majesty!' And Ḥallāj was put to death for saying: 'I am the Truth'.

The Sufis had already been on the defensive before this event. The second and third generations of Islam saw the birth of many heretical sects of different kinds, and the exoteric authorities, who were acutely conscious of the dangers of heresy, could by no means always discriminate between a conception of the religion that differed from theirs by way of deviation and one that differed from theirs by way of depth.[21] Moreover it was at this time that the Sufi orders were beginning to be formed, and where groups are concerned, suspicions are liable to be stronger and action is more likely to be taken. The adverse attention attracted towards Sufism by Ḥallāj's seven month trial and subsequent condemnation[22] was just what the Sufis themselves would have wished to avoid.[23]

[20] See Hujwīrī, *Kashf al-Maḥjūb*, pp. 184–6, and also 'Alī Ḥasan 'Abd al-Qādir, *The Life and Personality and Writings of Al-Junayd*, ch. IV.

[21] Many Western scholars appear to suffer from the same lack of discrimination, if we may judge from their use of the epithet 'orthodox'. In modern Orientalist parlance this precious and irreplaceable word comes dangerously near to being no more than a synonym of 'superficial' or 'exoteric'.

[22] In 922.

[23] Junayd, for example, more than once reproved his favourite disciple, Abū Bakr ash-Shiblī, for being too outspoken, and warned him against divulging the secrets of mysticism to those who had no right to know them (see Sarrāj, *Kitāb al-Luma'*, p. 234 in Nicholson's edition). Junayd's

But whatever its immediate effect may have been, his martyrdom was ultimately to prove a source of strength for the status of mystics and mysticism within the community as a whole. The verdict 'no man has a right to utter such words' has gradually come to be annulled in favour of the appeal 'man was not in this case the speaker'; and the utterance itself is now above all, for an increasing number of Muslims, an important part[24] of the evidence that Ḥallāj was one of the greatest Saints of Islam, while at the same time it serves as a general demonstration that the Sufis are not always directly responsible for what they say.

What Ḥallāj had virtually gained could only become effective on the basis of the more general recognition of Sufism which was built up gradually during the next 200 years. This was partly achieved by the simpler Sufi treatises[25] which were able to serve as bridges between the mystics and the community as a whole. But it is perhaps above all due to something which took place in the life of a very eminent exoteric authority of the latter half of the eleventh century, namely Ghazālī, who had an intense and providential experience of the necessity of Sufism. He experienced the truth that an intelligent soul, that is, one in which the higher reaches of the intelligence are in the process of awakening, cannot fail to see some of the many loose threads which the more outward exponents of the religion leave hanging, quite unknown to themselves. Failing the dimension of mysticism, such a

general attitude did not prevent him, however, from saying of Abū Yazīd al-Bistāmī: 'The rank of Abū Yazīd amongst us is even as that of Gabriel amongst the Angels' (Hujwīrī, *Kashf al-Maḥjūb*, ch. XII).

[24] *Veritas omnia vincit;* and the sum of what has come down to us about him—utterances, writings and features of his life—has too clear a ring of the Spirit to leave us in any doubt that here was a man directly conscious of being rooted in the Divine.

[25] Some of these are available in English, as for example Kalābādhī's *Ta'arruf* (*The Doctrine of the Sufis* in Arberry's translation) and Hujwīrī's *Kashf al-Maḥjūb* (translated by Nicholson).

soul will be in danger of passing judgement upon religion and hardening into scepticism, and this is what happened to Ghazālī. Having become one of the leading theologians and jurists of Baghdad he reached a point of crisis when, as he tells us, for a period of nearly two months he was in doubt about the truth of religion. It was a contact with Sufism that saved him; and his autobiographical treatise *The Saviour from Error*[26] is an affirmation of Sufism as the only reliable antidote to scepticism and as the highest aspect of the religion. His longest and best known work, *The Revival of the Sciences of the Religion*[27] was written as a means of reminding the whole community of the mystical bias which had characterized the Islam of the Prophet and his Companions. But not all his writings were written for everyone. In his treatise on the Divine Names[28] he goes so far as to say that the invocation of the Name *Allāh* is a means of deification (*ta'alluh*), and in his *Niche of Lights*[29] he expounds the doctrine of Oneness of Being with an altogether uncompromising directness.

If Ghazālī more than anyone else may be said to have prepared the way for the general recognition of Sufism, it was his younger contemporary, 'Abd al-Qādir al-Jīlānī (he was 33 at Ghazālī's death in 1111), who was to make the recognition fully operative. Like his predecessor, 'Abd al-Qādir had been something of an exoteric authority, and we are told that when he finally entered a Sufi order, some of his fellow initiates were inclined to resent the presence of a Ḥanbalī jurist in their midst. They little knew that for the next eight centuries and more—that is, down to the present day—this novice was destined to be known as 'the Sultan of

[26] *al-Munqidh min aḍ-ḍalāl*, translated by Montgomery Watt in *The Faith and Practice of Al-Ghazali* (Allen & Unwin, 1953).

[27] *Ihyā' 'ulūm ad-dīn:* many sections of this are available in English.

[28] *al-Maqṣad al-asnā.*

[29] *Mishkāt al-anwār*. (The English translation by Gairdner, published in 1924, was reprinted in 1952.)

the Saints'. It would perhaps be true to say that no one since the death of the Caliph 'Alī had exercised in person a spiritual influence of such far-reaching dimensions as did 'Abd al-Qādir. His inward gifts partly overflowed into the outward gift of an extraordinary eloquence, and over a period of years he gave mystical discourses in public near one of the gates of Baghdad. The were attended not only by Muslims but also by Jews and Christians, many of whom were converted by Sufism to Islam; and his order had spread to most parts of the Islamic world within one generation of his death.

The founding of the Qādirī *ṭarīqah* as a branch of the older Junaydī *ṭarīqah* into which 'Abd al-Qādir himself had been initiated was followed by the founding of branches of other older orders. The Chishtī *ṭarīqah*, founded by 'Abd al-Qādir's younger contemporary Mu'īn ad-Dīn Chishtī (d. 1236) has become one of the most widespread Sufi orders in India. To this age belongs also Jalāl ad-Dīn Rūmī (d. 1273) the greatest of Persian mystical poets, whose order the Mawlawī (Mevlevi) *ṭarīqah* has already been mentioned in connection with the sacred dance. But it is the *ṭarīqah* of Abū-Ḥasan ash-Shādhilī (d. 1258) that can best compare with that of 'Abd al-Qādir as regards amplitude which, in both cases, is far greater than it seems, since most of the variously named orders founded within the last 600 years are in fact derived from one or other of these two.

Abū Madyan Shu'ayb and Muḥyi 'd-Dīn ibn 'Arabī, who are also among the outstanding figures of this age, are no doubt the equals[30] in greatness of the four we have just mentioned. Abū Madyan was born in Seville, but later went to the East and was in Baghdad during the lifetime of 'Abd al-Qādir by whom he is said to have been invested with the

[30] The fact that Muḥyī 'd-Dīn is generally known as 'the Greatest Shaykh' suggests more, but although the Qādirīs and the Shādhilīs willingly allow him this title, they would certainly not allow him pre-eminence over their own great ancestors.

initiatic mantle (*khirqah*). Eventually he returned to the West and spent the last part of his life in Algeria, over which in a sense he still presides from his tomb outside Tlemcen.

Muḥyi 'd-Dīn ibn 'Arabī may be considered as an heir of Abū Madyan, for he was in close contact with several of his disciples and always speaks of him with extreme veneration, sometimes referring to him as 'my Shaykh'. Moreover, although they never actually met, the spiritual bond between them was confirmed, when Muḥyī 'd-Dīn was still a young man, by the grace of a miracle of levitation. He tells us that one evening he had just prayed the sunset prayer in his house in Seville when thoughts of Abū Madyan came into his mind and he felt a great longing to see him. Some minutes later, a man came in and greeted him, saying that he had just prayed the sunset prayer at Bugia in Algeria with Abū Madyan, who had told him to go at once to Ibn 'Arabī and tell him: 'As for our meeting together in the spirit, well and good, but as for our meeting in the flesh in this world, God will not permit it. Let him however rest assured, for the time appointed as a meeting for him and me lies in the security of God's mercy.'[31]

Another altogether outstanding spiritual heir of Abū Madyan was 'Abd as-Salām ibn Mashīsh, who likewise does not appear to have met him but was linked to him through an intermediary. Ibn Mashīsh was the master of Abū 'l-Ḥasan ash-Shādhilī, and together with Abū Madyan they span three generations as a triad which demonstrates—if indeed a demonstration should be necessary—the relative unimportance of the pen in Sufism. As regards writing they have left no more than a few poems, aphorisms and litanies[32] between

[31] *Sufis of Andalusia* (The *Rūḥ al-Quds* and *ad-Durrat al-Fākhirah*) translated by Ralph Austin (Allen & Unwin, 1971), p. 121.

[32] It must be admitted however that Ibn Mashīsh's poem in praise of the Prophet, *aṣ-Ṣalāt al-Mashīshiyyah* and Abū 'l-Ḥasan's incantation, *Ḥizb al-Baḥr*, are amongst the most often recited of all Sufi litanies.

them. Yet the certainty as to their spiritual magnitude is so unanimous amongst the Sufis of succeeding generations down to the present time that it would be perverse even for the most document-minded scholar to hold another opinion.

Their contemporary Muḥyi 'd-Dīn was on the other hand the most prolific of all Sufi writers. He insists however that this was not his intention but was always forced upon him. To write this or that work was his only means of achieving peace from the fire of the particular inspiration which drove him to write it, and he claims never to have written anything except under such a pressure. Being conscious of his own authority, he was afraid that writings not his would be fathered on him in years to come—a fear that has proved to be only too well founded—and not long before his death he drew up a list of his 270 works, divided into groups. One group consists of 'books which the All-Highest Truth commanded me, in my heart, to set down but which He hath not yet commanded me to bring forth to mankind'. Of these, 176 in number, only 16 have come down to us, and many of the writings which he did not deliberately withhold also appear to be lost. What has survived is nonetheless a treasury of prose and poetry which has exerted an untold influence on Sufism ever since. His most read and most commented work, *The Wisdom of the Prophets*[33] in 27 chapters, one for each Prophet, was 'given to him' in a single night when he was already 65. Here, as also elsewhere, he expounds the doctrine of Oneness of Being so explicitly and often so provocatively that some exoteric authorities, not to mention certain Western scholars, have wrongly supposed it to be his own particular and 'original' school of thought.

Others, concentrating on this work to the exclusion of his other writings, have equally wrongly classed him as a philosopher rather than a mystic.

[33] *Fuṣūṣ al-ḥikam.*

His longest surviving work, *The Meccan Revelations*,[34] so called because he was in Mecca when 'The Angel of inspiration' bade him begin it, consists of 565 chapters and is published in four large volumes. It is something of a miscellany, and in addition to what it contains about central doctrines of Sufism and about cosmological and other sciences which lie as it were at the margin of Sufism, it tells us much about the lives of his fellow mystics and is one of our chief sources of information about his own life. From this and one of two shorter treatises[35] we have the unescapable impression of a mystic in the fullest sense, a man of spiritual retreats and perpetual prayer, one who was recognised as a Saint in his lifetime and even in his youth, a visionary surpassed only by Prophets, and withal a man of tremendous spiritual presence, courted by kings and princes for his advice which was implacably and fearlessly outspoken. He was moreover destined to travel far and often,[36] and it was no doubt in the domain of personal contacts as much as through his writings, if not more, that he made himself felt during his life.

The essential feature of the period we are now considering was the recognition of Sufism as an integral part of Islam and a consequent repenetration of the community by Sufism insofar as this was possible in an age so full of exoteric 'crystal-

[34] *al-Futūḥāt al-makkiyyah*. A new edition is now being published in Cairo, edited by 'Uthmān Yaḥyà from the autograph manuscript he recently discovered.

[35] For example, his already quoted *Rūḥ al-Quds*. See also Seyyed Hossein Nasr, *Three Muslim Sages* (Cambridge, Mass., 1964).

[36] Like Abū Madyan he was an Andalusian, having been born in Murcia and brought up mainly in Seville. After several visits to North West Africa, he had a vision at the age of 33 in which he received a Divine Command to go to the East. There, after much travelling and longer or shorter periods of rest in various places—Cairo, Mecca, Baghdad, Mosul, Konya, Aleppo and others—he finally settled in Damascus, where he died in 1240. A mosque was built over his tomb in the sixteenth century by the Ottoman Sultan Salīm II.

lisations' which had not been there at the outset. The following formulation, by an eminent fourteenth-century jurist,[37] may be said to express what had now come to be generally accepted: 'The sciences of the religion are three: jurisprudence (*fiqh*) which is referred to in the Tradition reported by the son of 'Umar[38] as *islām* (submission), the theological principles (*uṣūl ad-dīn*),[39] which are referred to as *īmān* (faith), and mysticism (*taṣawwuf*) which is referred to as *iḥsān* (excellence). As to anything else, it must either be reduced to one of these denominations, or otherwise it is outside the religion'.[40]

Recognition demands in return accessibility which involves organisation; and the spread of the orders and their increasing openness, which enabled the 'heart's blood' to flow more freely throughout the 'body' of Islam as a whole, could have been detrimental to the quality of Islamic mysticism but for the understanding that its accessibility can never be total. It is perhaps not without interest to quote here a piece of advice about Sufism given to Muslim students by an early nineteenth-century rector of the Azhar University in Cairo, since to be head of Islam's chief centre of learning is to be something of an authority for the whole Islamic world:

[37] Tāj ad-Dīn as-Subkī.

[38] 'Umar, the second caliph had been present on the occasion of its utterance and had transmitted it later to his son. It is usually known as the Tradition of Gabriel because in it the Prophet defined the three planes of the religion in answer to questions put to him by the Archangel. He answered the question 'What is *islām?*' by mentioning the 'five pillars' (see above, p. 74) and the question 'what is *īmān?*' by formulating the Islamic *credo* (p. 22) His answer to 'what is *iḥsān?*' has already been given (p. 58). For a translation of this basic Tradition, see *A Sufi Saint of the Twentieth Century*, pp. 44–5.

[39] Literally 'the principles of the religion' but the context shows that the reference here is to the principles of what must be believed (as distinct from what must be done).

[40] The above passage is translated from a quotation which only gives the author but not the actual treatise in which it occurs.

'The lore of Sufism falls into two categories. One of these is concerned with disciplining the character and investing it with all the spiritual courtesies, and to this category belong such books as Ghazālī's *Iḥyā'*. . . . This lore is as clear as day, and is within the grasp of anyone who has the slightest application to learning. In the other category the masters of Sufism are concerned with mysteries being unveiled and with direct spiritual perceptions and what they experience by way of Divine Manifestations, as in the writings of Muhyi 'd-Dīn ibn 'Arabī and Jīlī[41] and others of their bent. This lore is too abstruse for anyone to understand who has not shared their experience in some degree. Moreover it may happen that their manner of expression does not adequately convey their meaning, and if taken literally if may conflict with all logical evidence. It is therefore better not to pry into it, but to leave its masters to enjoy their own privileged states.'[42]

The author does not mention Ḥallāj by name, but he would almost certainly have been thinking of him in connection with the closing remarks; for if it was not due to Ḥallāj that Sufism came to be recognised as necessary to Islam, it would no doubt be true to say that while being so recognised it was all the more able to obtain the recognition of its right to an aspect of exclusiveness and mystery because in Ḥallāj that aspect was unmistakeably and unescapably there as a fact, personified no longer merely by relatively hidden recluses but by a lasting celebrity whose case was retried by every generation and with regard to whom there was an increasing consciousness of collective guilt to be expiated.

[41] See above, p. 70. The reference here is probably above all to his poem *al-'Ayniyyah* which is partly edited and translated in Appendix I of Nicholson's *Studies in Islamic Mysticism*.

[42] Ḥasan ibn Muḥammed al-'Attār *Ḥāshiyah* (supercommentary) on *Jam' al-Jawāmi'* by Tāj ad-Dīn as-Subkī.

Circles within circles within circles is a structure from which in the nature of things, no mysticism can escape; and the more recognition a mysticism receives and the more it is organised, the clearer cut that structure will become. In addition to its most central members and to those who are initiates but not 'travellers', every great Sufi order has at its fringe a large number—sometimes even thousands—of men and women who, without being formally initiated, seek the blessing and guidance of the Shaykh as regards the performance of voluntary worship in addition to what is obligatory. Such guidance often includes the transmission of a litany for regular recitation; and through its litanies Sufism penetrates the outer world of Islam to an extent which can partly be measured by the fact that *Dalā 'il al-Khayrāt*, a manual of invocations of blessings on the Prophet compiled by a Shādhili Shaykh in the fifteenth century is perhaps, after the Qur'ān itself, the most widely distributed book in Islam. Referring in general to this overflow of Sufism—to its function, we might say, as the heart of the religion—a modern western authority on Islamic prayer-manuals writes:

> 'In purchasing the books (of devotions) it was my desire to avoid the more esoteric works for the inner life of the dervish orders, and enquiry was made as to what had a popular sale. Even so, the majority of the books proved to be linked with one or other of the orders that have played, and still in these days of their official submergence[43] play,

[43] In seeking a total secularisation of the Turkish state, Ataturk found that the firmest resistance came from the Sufi orders, whereupon he outlawed them and put to death many of their leaders. But what suffered most, as the above quotation implies, was the fringe. To make Sufism illegal is to disperse the outer circle or circles and to prevent the nucleus from any manifest radiation but not from carrying on its own essential spiritual work. A similar attempt to abolish Sufism, but for puritanical not anti-religious motives, was made by the Wahhābīs when they gained control of Saudi Arabia. Here again, it is the outward manifestations of

so great a part in the life of Islam. Indeed it seems almost impossible for a man seeking for instruction in prayer, beyond directions for the daily prayer rite, to avoid works connected with one or other of the orders. Since these became illegal in Turkey there is a dearth of devotional material in Istanbul, once so rich a centre.'[44]

Another way in which Sufism overflows into outer Islam is through its dead—and this shows perhaps more clearly than anything else the central status of Sufism within the religion as a whole. A living Saint belongs first of all to his disciples and then secretly, through his presence, to the community as a whole. But dead, his presence is no longer secret; and there is scarcely a region in the empire of Islam which has not a Sufi for its Patron Saint. Needless to say, not all the greatest have drawn devotion to themselves in equal measure,[45]

Sufism that have been suppressed. But Mecca and Medina still continue to be the two great meetings places for Sufis from all over the Islamic world.

[44] Constance Padwick, *Muslim Devotations* (S.P.C.K., 1961), pp. xi–xii.

[45] As might be expected, Baghdad is particularly favoured in its dead. One of its earliest Sufi tombs is that of Bishr al-Ḥāfī (see above, p. 77), whose celebrity was guaranteed by a Divine promise at the very outset of his spiritual path, which is said to have begun as follows. He saw one day a piece of paper lying in the mud at the side of the road, and his eye fell on the Divine Name which occurred in the sentences that were written upon it. He took it up, cleaned it, bought some scent, perfumed it, and placed it in a cavity of the wall of his house; and that night he heard a voice say to him: 'O Bishr, thou has made fragrant My Name in this world and I will make thine fragrant in this world and the next.' In contrast to the simple and intimate tomb of Bishr is the great mosque across the river beneath whose golden dome lies the sepulchre of Musà 'l-Kāẓim, great grandson of a great grandson of the Prophet. For the Shī'ī minority he is the seventh of the twelve Imams, to whom they attribute a prolongation of the Prophetic function. But he is venerated as a Saint by the whole community of Islam, and the Sufis trace through him one of their lines of spiritual descent from the Prophet. Within easy walking distance from his mosque is the much smaller one which houses

but the tombs of many of those mentioned in this book, and of many others not mentioned, are shrines of pilgrimage[46] from near and from far.

The last quotation has brought us to the present century sooner than was intended. To revert for a moment to the period which immediately followed the great crystallisation of the Sufi orders, mention must be made of two works which have the extreme importance of being amongst those which are most often consulted and quoted and meditated upon in the inner circles of Sufism. The first of these is *al-Ḥikam* (literally 'the wisdoms'), a collection of aphorisms written by Ibn 'Aṭā' Allāh al-Iskandarī[47] at the end of the thirteenth century.[48] The last element of his name denotes that he was from Alexandria, which was one of the earliest centres of the Shādhilī

the tomb of his spiritual grandson Ma'rūf al-Karkhī—a sanctuary renowned as a *tiryāq* (theriac, antidote), because so many sicknesses have been cured there. Ma'rūf was the freed slave and disciple of the son and successor of Musà 'l-Kāẓim, namely 'Alī ar-Riḍā, the eighth Shī'ī Imam who, from his sepulchre at Meshhed, may be said to preside over the whole of Persia. But in Ma'rūf two spiritual chains meet, for he was also the disciple and successor of the already mentioned Dāwud aṭ-Ṭā'ī; and in one of the cemeteries near to Ma'rūf's mosque is a large shrine in which Sufis often hold sessions of remembrance, drawn to that place by a double blessing, for there are two tombs in this sanctuary, that of Sarī as-Saqaṭī, disciple and successor of Ma'rūf, and that of Junayd. Any one of those we have mentioned here is great enough in himself to be the spiritual centre of the city; and if none of them is considered as its Patron Saint, it is simply because—to go back once more across the Tigris—the tomb of 'Abd al-Qādir is perhaps, after that of the Prophet and those of certain members of his family, the most visited and venerated tomb in Islam. Even in far off Morocco 'Sidi Baghdad' (my Lord Baghdad) is none other than 'Abd al-Qādir al-Jīlānī.

[46] See *Religion in the Middle East* (Cambridge University Press, 1969), vol. 2, pp. 266–7.

[47] d. 1309.

[48] They have just been published in English, under the title of *Sufi Aphorisms*, translated with an introduction and notes by Victor Danner (E. J. Brill, Leiden) 1973.

ṭarīqah.[49] To this day the town's most holy monument is the mosque which enshrines the tomb of Abū 'l-'Abbās al-Mursī, the successor of the founder of that order. Ibn 'Aṭa' Allāh was the disciple of Abū 'l-'Abbās, and there can be little doubt that these aphorisms constitute, if only indirectly, an important part of our legacy from the great Abū 'l-Ḥasan himself.

The second of these texts, which belongs to the early fifteenth century, is the already referred to *al-Insān al-kāmil* (Universal Man) by 'Abd al-Karīm al-Jīlī[50]—a remarkably clear, concentrated and profound exposition of Sufi doctrine.

Until recently most scholars were inclined to agree that Jīlī was the last great mystic of Islam. As regards the intervening period between his time and ours, it would have been freely admitted that there are one or two who come near to greatness—for example, Aḥmad Zarrūq,[51] who was considered by his contemporaries, especially in Libya where he spent the last part of his life, as the Ghazālī of his day. Modern scholarship is also aware, but admittedly without having done justice to him, of 'Abd al-Ghanī an-Nābulusī[52] who, in addition to being the author of profound commentaries on the *Fuṣūṣ al-Ḥikam* of Ibn 'Arabī and on the *Khamriyyah* (Wine-Song) of Ibn al-Fāriḍ, was himself a true poet.[53] But such figures have not been able to save this period as a whole from the cumulative condemnation which Western scholars have pronounced upon it, one echoing another.

[49] The first centre was (and still is) at Tunis, but after having founded his order there, Abū'l-Ḥasan moved to Alexandria.

[50] See above pp. 70 and 117. Only parts of this treatise are as yet available in English, translated by Nicholson in his *Studies in Islamic Mysticism.* Other parts are available in French, translated by Titus Burckhardt, *De l'Homme Universel* (P. Derain, Lyon, 1953).

[51] d. 1493. A study of him has recently been written by the Libyan scholar Aḥmad al-Ḥushaymī, but has not yet been published.

[52] d. 1731.

[53] See his remarkable lines on the symbolism of letters and ink, quoted in *A Sufi Saint of the Twentieth Century*, pp. 150–1.

The Western world has for so long been under the domination of humanism that writers about Sufism sometimes unconsciously pass judgement upon it according to humanistic and therefore anti-mystical standards. We are brought up to believe that from about the sixteenth century onwards the East began to 'stagnate', whereas the West 'developed' and 'progressed'. But it is practically always forgotten that whatever this last word may mean, there is one thing it is never intended to mean, even by the most fanatical of progressists, and this is 'progress in other-worldliness'—the only kind of progress which mysticism can recognise. As regards the charge of 'stagnation', this means in the case of Sufism that it has not produced 'original thinkers', which brings us back to our opening chapter. If the word original be taken here in its modern sense, then this supposed weakness is a strength—the firmness of not being side-tracked into manifestations of individualism in which novelty takes precedence over truth. But as to originality in the true sense, that is, direct contact with the Origin, its perpetuation is the theme of the already quoted promise: 'The earth shall not be found lacking in forty men whose hearts are as the heart of the Friend of the All-Merciful', for the Arabic *khalīl* (friend) denotes intimate contact or, more precisely, interpenetration.[54] We may quote also the Tradition: 'God will send unto this people at the head of every hundred years one who will renew for it its religion', for there can be no renewal of vigour without a return to the source of inspiration. For the Sufi these promises guarantee fulfilment. Western scholars,

[54] Very relevant are the last two lines of a poem attributed to Rābi'ah al-'Adawiyyah which may be translated (sacrificing poetry to the needs of our context):

'Wherever life threads its way throughout my being, there Thou hast penetrated (*takhallalta*), and that is why a *khalīl* is called a *khalīl*.'

For the whole poem in a translation which aims at avoiding the above sacrifice, see *A Sufi Saint of the Twentieth Century*, p. 180.

on the other hand, will be more concerned with what they would call the objective evidence. But are they capable of assessing it? Not that they fail to grasp the traditional conception of originality; men like Nicholson, Massignon and Arberry understood very well in principle what is meant by this, and though their thinking was liable to be confused by unconscious and probably not very deep-rooted prejudices in favour of the modern parody, it was beyond doubt true originality that they looked for and appreciated in the great Sufis. But although they were right in supposing it to be the inevitable result of spiritual greatness, and therefore a criterion of it, what they did not understand enough—or what they sometimes forgot—was that the manifestations of direct contact with the Origin are infinitely varied. In other words, their conception of true originality was too narrow, nor could they always be relied on to recognise it in all its forms.

This however is only a secondary cause of the injustice which we are considering.[55] As regards the primary cause, it has to be admitted that the semi-official verdict of Orientalism on latter century Sufism is mainly based on inadequate information. Sufism is by its nature secret, and it may take time for its depths to become manifest, whereas the scum[56] rises at once to the surface. Arberry for example spoke of

[55] Another secondary cause is their attentiveness and subservience to the opinions of modernist Orientals. Yet another, their failure to remember that though writings can be exceptionally, a 'proof' of spiritual greatness—as in the case of Junayd, Ḥallāj, Ibn 'Arabī and Jīlī, for example—lack of writings proves nothing at all, either one way or other.

[56] In 1934 (*Encylopaedia of Islam*) Massignon wrote of the orders: 'The acrobatics and juggling practised by certain adepts of the lower classes, and the moral corruption of too many of their leaders has aroused against almost all of them the hostility and contempt of the élite of the modern Muslim world'. One is however tempted to suspect that the above use of the word 'élite' will not stand too close an examination.

Sufism as being already in the sixteenth century 'in its death-throes', and he generalised so far as to maintain: 'Though the Sufi Orders continued—and in many countries continue—to hold the interest and allegiance of the ignorant masses, no man of education would care to speak in their favour.'[57] Yet when his attention was subsequently drawn to the Shaykh Aḥmad al-'Alawī who only died in 1934, he freely admitted that here was a man 'whose sanctity recalled the golden age of mediaeval mystics'.[58] Other scholars have made similar pronouncements[59] about him; and it can be affirmed without fear of contradiction that his treatise on the symbolism of the letters of the alphabet is one of the most profound texts in all Sufi literature. Moreover—and this is extremely important in the present context—his brief yet enthralling account of his own spiritual path gives us to believe that his own Shaykh, Muḥammad al-Būzīdī, was also like himself a great spiritual guide. It is not a question of filial piety. The Shaykh al-'Alawī

[57] *Sufism*, p. 122. It must not be forgotten however that the voice of 'the ignorant masses' is sometimes *vox dei*. Moreover an illiterate Bedouin can be, in himself, exceedingly shrewd, and he sometimes has spontaneous powers of physiognomy which are very much to the point in the present context, and which are not to be learned at school. On the other hand, if it be asked precisely why the modern oriental 'man of education' would not care to speak in favour of the Sufi orders, will the true answer be: 'Because he is enlightened'? Or will it be: 'Objectively, because the innermost circles of Sufism are altogether hidden from him and, subjectively, because he does not wish to be thought naïve, superstitious and backward'?

[58] This needs to be recorded and remembered as modification of the many far too sweeping strictures that devalue the last chapter of his above mentioned little book which is, in all its other chapters, of lasting value as a rich anthology of remarkable quotations from Sufi texts.

[59] L. O. Schumann refers to him as 'that really great man, the Algerian Shaykh'. Arnold Hottinger speaks of him as 'a true and great mystic' and adds that he cannot read of him 'without an overwhelming sense of the loss—perhaps a fatal one—that would afflict Islam if such men should entirely disappear'.

was too objective, with too much sense of the rights of truth, particularly as regards so important a question as spiritual status,[60] to allow sentiment to cloud his judgement. Nor in fact does he set about praising his Shaykh; he simply tells us what he said and did; and the result, as far as we are concerned, is not merely the impression but the certainty that here was a true master of souls. Yet the Shaykh al-Būzīdī left no writings and is unknown to Western scholarship—or was so until very recently. His own Shaykh has been equally neglected, Muḥammad ibn Qaddūr al-Wakīlī, who was also clearly a man of spiritual eminence. The Shaykh al-Būzīdī used to tell his disciples how he had found this master through the blessing of a remarkable vision in which the great Abū Madyan had appeared to him and told him to go from Algeria to Morocco. This takes us back, all but one link in the chain, to the founder of the Darqāwī order himself, for Muḥammad ibn Qaddūr was the spiritual grandson of Mūlāy[61] al-'Arabī ad-Darqāwī, 'the Shaykh of our Shaykhs' as he is called by so many Sufis of North-West Africa and elsewhere, even to the present day. The letters of this Sufi master have already been quoted in

[60] One of the characteristics of the modern East, which may be said to apply to Hinduism as much as to Sufism, is the wilful confusing of outward function with inward realization, rather as if, in the West, it were to be assumed that because a man is Pope he is therefore a Saint. It is true that a man who is legitimate acting head of a Sufi order has in fact certain powers of guidance provided that he keep strictly, as regards method, to his traditional patrimony. But only one who has himself reached the End of the path is a spiritual guide in the full sense of the Arabic term *murshid*, and the Shaykh al-'Alawī was conscious of the numbers of Sufi dignitaries in his day who, out of wishful thinking aggravated no doubt by the wishful thinking of their followers, claimed to be adepts. A remarkable passage in one of his poems consists of lines addressed by him to an impostor, interrogating him about his inward state.

[61] Moroccan dialect form of *mawlay* (my lord), a title used in Morocco to denote an eminent descendant of the Prophet.

earlier chapters;[62] and like the 'Alawī autobiography they leave us with no less than certainty that the author's Shaykh, Mūlāy 'Alī al-Jamal, was also a great master. Indeed, it would be no exaggeration to say that we have here, in this spiritual line, two pairs of successive Shaykhs—'Alī al-Jamal and al-'Arabī ad-Darqāwī, then after two generations Muḥammad al-Būzīdī and Aḥmad al-'Alawī—who are the equals of their ninth-century ancestors Sarī and Junayd; and in all three cases there seems little doubt that the second of each pair was, for his century, the 'renewer' promised by the Prophet.[63] The disparities lie, not in the renewers themselves, but their respective settings. There is no denying that the general level of spirituality was far higher in the earlier centuries than in the later ones. Junayd was like a summit surrounded by other summits and gentle slopes; but though the summits of Sufism remain as constants, undiminished in height, they become fewer in number, while the surrounding slopes grow steeper and steeper.

The Shaykh ad-Darqāwī had nonetheless many remarkable disciples, some of whom he recognised during his lifetime as autonomous Shaykhs.[64] But as might be expected, his letters tell us not so much about his posterity as about his ancestry. In fact one of their most striking characteristics is that they make us and keep us conscious of what might be called the vibrations of the spiritual chain of succession in virtue of the many and masterly quotations which the author gives us from his ancestors.

[62] See above, pp. 21 (note 6), 66–8. These epistles, written to various disciples, provide an example of a true originality which Western scholars long failed to recognise as such.

[63] Both the Shaykh ad-Darqawi and the Shaykh al-'Alawi were conscious of having this function and of being moreover each the spiritual Axis (*quṭb*) of his time. See *A Sufi Saint*, p. 224, ll. 17–18.

[64] See the preface to *Letters of a Sufi Master*, and also *L'Autobiographie du Soufi Marocain Aḥmad ibn 'Ajībah* translated with introduction etc. by J.-L. Michon (E. J. Brill, 1969).

Many of the Shaykhs who form the links of this and other spiritual chains which span the centuries from the eighteenth back into the fourteenth and beyond have left writings which only exist in a few manuscripts[65] and are so far unknown to Western scholars. But there are signs that efforts are now being made in the East as well as in the West to recover something of this heritage; and it might be fitting, even at the risk of abruptness, to close the present chapter, and with it the book, on this note of expectancy. But it must never be forgotten that writings are not an essential feature of Sufism. The basic question to be asked in the context of these last paragraphs is not: How many important Sufi treatises have been written in the last few centuries? It is: Has Sufism continued to be an operative means, for man, of reintegration in his Divine Origin? And while it may be true that less and less men are capable of taking advantage of all that Sufism has to offer, there can be no doubt that the answer to this last question is in the affirmative.

[65] For example, *ar-Rasā'il al-Jamaliyyah*, the letters of the Shaykh ad-Darqāwī's master. Extracts from these are often read aloud during the *majālis* of the Darqāwī order, especially in one group which congregates regularly at the tomb of the author in Fez. But they have never been published.

Index of Persons[1], Book Titles (in italics), Places, etc.

[1] As regards the pronunciation of Arabic, *ḥ* is a tensely breathed *h* sound; *ḍ, ṣ, ṭ, ẓ* are pronounced somewhat heavily, far back in the mouth; *q* is a guttural *k* sound; *th* is like *th* in *think*, *dh* like *th* in this, *gh* like a French *r*, *kh* like *ch* in Scottish *loch*; ' stands for the letter *'ayn* which is produced by narrowing the passage in the depth of the throat and then forcing the breath through it. ' in the middle and at the end of a word stands for *hamzah* which marks a break of continuity in the breath. Since in English initial vowel sounds are regularly pronounced with a *hamzah*, the initial *hamzah* has not been transcribed here, e.g., *Aḥmad*, not *'Aḥmad.* ' at the beginning of a word is an apostrophe indicating an elided vowel, e.g. *bismi 'Llāh* (the first vowel of the Divine Name *Allāh* is always elided except at the beginning of a sentence or when the Name stands alone).

The short vowels a, i, u are like the vowel sounds of *sat, sit, soot*; *ā* (or *á*, so written to indicate a difference of Arabic spelling but not of pronunciation) is like the vowel sound of *bare*, but back consonants next to it attract it to that of *bar*; *ī* and *ū* are like the vowel sounds of *seen* and *soon*; *ay* is between those of *sign* and *sane*; *aw* is like that of *cow*.

[2] Persons are listed under their family names unless they are better known by their first name, as here, or by some other name.

Index of Arabic Words

(except book titles and names of persons and places)